Armenia at the Crossroads
Democracy and Nationhood in the Post-Soviet Era

*Essays, interviews, and speeches by
the leaders of the national democratic movement in Armenia*

Edited by

Gerard J. Libaridian

Blue Crane Books
Watertown, Massachusetts

Armenia at the Crossroads
Democracy and Nationhood in the Post-Soviet Era
Essays, interviews, and speeches by
the leaders of the national democratic movement in Armenia

Edited by Gerard J. Libaridian

Published by Blue Crane Books
A division of Arrow Graphics, Inc. Watertown, Massachusetts
   in cooperation with Libner Enterprises

Copyright © 1991 by Gerard J. Libaridian. All rights reserved

Cover design by Aramais Andonian
Cover photograph *Leninakan, Armenia 1989*, by Bérge Ara Zobian
Documents translated and annotated by Gerard J. Libaridian

Typography and electronic pagination by Arrow Graphics, Inc.
   Watertown, Massachusetts

Printed in the United States of America

Library of Congress Cataloging-in-Publication Data

Armenia at the crossroads : democracy and nationhood in the post-Soviet era : essays, interviews, and speeches by the leaders of the national democratic movement in Armenia / edited by Gerard J. Libaridian.
      p.   cm.
      Includes bibliographical references.
      1. Armenian S.S.R.—History—Autonomy and independence movements—Sources. 2. Nationalism—Armenian S.S.R.—History—Sources. 3. Soviet Union—Politics and government—1985-   I. Libaridian, Gerard J.
DK686.9.A75 1991   91-70342
947'.92—dc20   CIP
ISBN 0-9628715-1-6 (hc)
ISBN 0-9628715-0-8 (pb)

*To Victor Ayvazian
and all
democrats and patriots
in today's Armenia
who, with their lives
and their deaths, are
making peaceful change
and democracy possible*

Contents

Preface — *vii*

Introduction — *1*

Documents

Document One — *9*
  The Law of Excluding the Third Force
  Rafael Ishkhanian

Document Two — *39*
  Four Questions to Vazgen Manukian

Document Three — *47*
  The Riga Meetings
  Hambartsum Galstyan

Document Four — *51*
  It Is Time to Jump off the Train
  Vazgen Manukian

Document Five — *87*
  Interview with Ktrich Sardarian

Document Six — *95*
  Statement of Levon Ter Petrosian Armenian National Movement Candidate for the Presidency of the Armenian Supreme Soviet

Document Seven — *107*
  Declaration on Armenia's Independence by the Parliament of Armenia

Document Eight — *111*
  The State of the Republic
  Levon Ter Petrosian

Document Nine — *119*
  The State of the Union
  Levon Ter Petrosian

Appendices

Appendix A:
Democracy and Diaspora Politics

Appendix A-One   127
Joint Statement by the Three Armenian
Political Parties in the Diaspora

Appendix A-Two   130
The Fatherland and the Diaspora

Appendix B:
The Idea of Independence and Its Protectors

Appendix B-One   137
Toward the Dawn of Freedom
With an Independent Politics
Khajak Ter Grigorian

Appendix B-Two   143
We Must Cherish the Vision of a Free,
Independent, and United Armenia
Hrair Maroukhian

Appendix C:
Pan-Turkism, Democracy, and Independence

Appendix C-One   149
Pan-Turkism and the Armenian Question
The Twenty-Fourth World Congress of the
Dashnaktsutiune

Appendix C-Two   151
The Threat of Pan-Turanism
Zori Balayan

Appendix C-Three   155
Pan-Turanism: A Response
from the Karabagh Committee

Postscript   157
Democracy, Diaspora, and the
National Agenda
Gerard J. Libaridian

Preface

This project was undertaken as a simple exercise in gathering documents that could introduce the position of the national democratic movement in Armenia led by the Karabagh Committee on a variety of issues.

As the work progressed, it became obvious that the political thinking of the movement leadership represented more than a series of "demands" or grievances. Strengthened by a refreshing reinterpretation of history and freed from burdensome nationalistic or ideological orthodoxies, the analyses and direction of the members and associates of the Karabagh Committee amounted to a coherent articulation of a new agenda for the Armenian nation based on new strategic principles of survival: decolonization, sovereignty, and nation-building through self-reliance, redefinition of national interests, realistic assessment of one's geo-political environment, and good neighborly relations with all neighbors; and democratization.

The new strategy is significant for Armenia and Armenians for a number of reasons. With rare exceptions, Armenian political thinking during the past many centuries had sought to achieve national goals through reliance on foreign forces. National interests were therefore redefined to fit the assumed needs of interested foreigners.

The new strategy also surfaced at a time when diaspora Armenian political processes had reached a dead end. The movement challenged the Soviet system and the Soviet empire just as Armenian community thinking abroad had come to accept a Soviet Armenia as inevitable. In a fatalistic world, the inevitable ultimately becomes justifiable, even desirable.

The authors of these documents—the leaders of the movement—also seemed to share with some diasporan intellectuals the mistrust toward uses and misuses of the Genocide in contemporary Armenian society. A shared distrust of fear and of strategy based on fear generated by the Genocide was essential in fostering, for the first time since Sovietization, the real participation of diaspora Armenians in the "building" of Armenia. These parallels were as unsettling as they were gratifying. They did make it possible for the two segments of the Armenian nation to cooperate because of basic shared values and outlooks rather than because of convenience or absence of alternatives. The editor of this volume was one of those who shared those values.

The work turned into a labor of love and discovery. Begun in March 1990, its birth was delayed as events unfolded. At the end of 1989 the Karabagh Committee organized the Armenian National Movement by bringing together a large number of reform oriented groups. In May 1990, the Armenian National Movement became the Parliament of Armenia. In August of the same year the movement took over the government.

The main part of the volume is limited to documents emanating directly from the movement and some of its leaders. The coherence of the movement is to be found in the ability of its leaders to ask, in a systematic manner, a set of critical questions regarding the past, present, and future of the Armenian nation. Hence the single most important criterion for the selection of documents: their ability to elucidate the fundamental dimensions of the movement's thinking. Some pieces—such as the article by Rafael Ishkhanian, the second document by Vazgen Manukian, the speeches by Levon Ter Petrosian, and the Parliament's Declaration on Independence—stand out as critical on first reading. The importance of others is revealed by time.

The Appendices introduce the views of others as well. Hopefully this will not only further enlighten the position of the movement but also place its thinking within a larger political spectrum. In this respect, the volume does not reflect, unfortunately, the views of all the political groups currently functioning among Armenians. A second edition will certainly correct this defect. Nonetheless, the selections cover the substance of positions on the major issues currently being debated by Armenians and others interested in Armenia.

During the preparation of this volume many of the names used underwent changes. For Armenians, Karabagh was renamed Artsakh, its historical name. The Karabagh Committee, short for the Karabagh Movement Armenia Committee, continues to exist, although most of its organizational functions have been absorbed by the Armenian National Movement it engendered. Armenia's Supreme Soviet—its elected national legislative body—is occasionally referred to as Supreme Council or

Parliament. The translations reflect the names used in the original texts.

A comment on the title of the volume. The term post-Soviet seemed at first premature, at best uncertain. Yet, upon reflection, one can argue that whatever follows, the "Soviet" era of Russian imperialism is over. This is best reflected by the decision of the Parliament of Armenia to delete the word from the name of the country and rename it the Republic of Armenia. More than the legal terminology, however, one realizes that we are witnessing the end of an era. Even if the the union survives its current crises or is transformed into a looser confederation, it will be difficult to return to a word which, as justification for imperialism abroad and totalitarianism at home is altogether discredited within Russia itself.

I am deeply grateful to all my colleagues and co-workers at the Zoryan Institute who, throughout the past nine years, have given much to make this and other projects possible.

G.J.L.
1991

Introduction

This volume considers a simple question: Can Armenia be an independent state? To be more explicit one can ask, Can Armenia achieve strategic and political viability as a sovereign state capable of defining and managing its own vital interests or does her survival mandate continuing as a vassal state of an imperial power in return for protection?

It is possible to deal with the question by focusing on the overwhelming interdependence of contemporary states to the extent that intelligent discourse can be sustained only when independence is understood in relative terms. That will be an inadequate context, however, for the understanding of the issue for two reasons.

Interdependence—whether strategic or economic—does not deny governments the right to define national interests and a national agenda for the people they govern, to set priorities, and to determine the cost they are willing to pay to achieve a given goal, considering the resources available to them within their own borders, their ability to defend their interests, and to realize their agenda.

Second, the problem presents itself to the Armenian people in a particular context. For too long the fear of neighbors has been the most dominant factor in determining the answer to the question of Armenian independence. Engendered by a series of massacres and a genocide in the twentieth century, strengthened by the imagery of the brutal Turk, nurtured by the surviving specter of Pan-Turkism, internalized as the psychology of the victim and the colonized, manipulated by Armenia's self-appointed protectors, that fear has, in fact, distorted the perception of national interests, and has been confused with strategic thinking.

That fear has been legitimized by Armenians' self-definition as a special people, endowed with a special mission in the region, if not in the world. True, occasionally Armenians' definition of their land as a "Christian island in a sea of Muslims" has been modified as "an outpost of Western civilization surrounded by backwardness" or, for the politically inspired, a natural defender of Russia's interests in the Caucasus. Throughout these changes, however, the need for an outside protector has remained the foundation of what passes for strategic thinking; all other concerns have been subordinated to the need to acquire and please that protector. As a result, missionary zeal and readiness for martyrdom—proof of moral superiority—have replaced a political agenda, while a sense of impotence and rush to self-denigration have been mistaken for political realism.

The Genocide, its exploitation, and its denial by Turkey have paralyzed the collective psyche of the Armenian people. A nation of victims—at first, of the violence, and subsequently of its denial—is incapable of sustaining a rational discourse. A nation cannot imagine a future if the only thing it can imagine the future bringing is further victimization. The denial of the future justifies the denial of the present and mandates an obsessive treatment of an overburdened past. Under the circumstances, the function of history is merely to chronicle and legitimize this fear.

This fear—both justified and imagined—of the Turk, the Muslim, Pan-Turkism, pogroms, massacres and a new genocide has been exploited and manipulated to rationalize, even welcome, the lack of independence and absence of democracy in Armenia. The predominance of a threat to the nation's existence—a sort of permanent state of war—mandated the acceptance of the protection brought by Russia's incorporation of Armenia. So went the argument.

The national democratic movement, first known as the Karabagh Movement, led by the Karabagh Committee and institutionalized by the Armenian National Movement (ANM), questioned the validity of the paradigm based on fear, raised serious doubts on the imminence of a Pan-Turkic danger, reestablished the right to determine a national agenda, and reintroduced rational discourse as the means to answer questions.

The texts introduced in this volume provide a tentative answer to the question of an alternative strategy of survival. The answer is provided through the writings of some of the leading members of Armenia's national democratic movement. Beginning with public demonstrations, in late 1987, against the state's disastrous environmental policies, Armenia's perestroika-inspired protest movement engulfed most of the population of the republic in February 1988 in support of Armenians' right for self-determination in Azerbaijani controlled Mountainous Karabagh. By May 1988, the movement, now clearly led by the Karabagh Committee, had reached the conclusion that without radical political change none of these or other issues—despotism, economic disintegration, corruption, bureaucratism, arbitrariness, culture, etc.—could be resolved satisfactorily. From then on, the movement turned into a peaceful revolution steered by the Karabagh Committee and led by the ANM. This phase of the history of the movement ended with the victory of the ANM-led coalition of democratic forces in national parliamentary elections and the formation of an ANM government in August 1990.

These texts were not intended as philosophical writings. They are articles, interviews, speeches, produced in the heat of the struggle. Yet they represent a coherent body of thought. They bear the stamp of a coherence that has evolved through a process of critical analysis that must have engaged a number of the current participants and leaders of the movement. These pieces articulate conclusions which, in order to be shared by the authors, must have evolved through intense debates over a period of time and must have been tested by the extremely varied and trying conditions imposed on Armenia during the past three years.

The body of thought suggested by these writings can be summarized in the following way. Armenians must recognize that membership in the Soviet Union has meant the discarding of a national agenda, the destruction of a value system, and the subordination to a logic which had very little to do with the interests of the citizens of the republic either as Armenians or as citizens. The Soviet Union has particularly failed in the one area which had been accepted as a religious belief: lack of independence and democracy had to be accepted in return for the physical protection of Armenians from imminent or potential threat from neighbors and from Pan-Turkism. Sumgait and other pogroms against Armenians in Azerbaijan from 1988 to 1990 proved otherwise. This logic is not sustained by political analysis alone, the volume would indicate. Armenians have adopted a distorted view of their past that blinded them too long to the realities of the present. A critical view of history does not support, argue the authors, the simplistic view that Armenians have been only helpless victims of genocide and can only be victims again if left to their own devices.

While Pan-Turkism is an ideology relevant for our understanding of the First World War events, it is currently a functionally irrelevant program. Moreover, the assumption or argument that in case of independence Pan-Turkism is the operative principle which will guide Armenia's neighbors or that it is the ideology which explains current changes in the USSR is, at best, unproven. Pan-Turkism, has concluded the ANM, is the scarecrow which distorts the nation's view of the past, obscures other, real issues today, and denies Armenians the right to imagine the future, thus serving the interests of Russian imperialism alone.

The argument is carried further by connecting democracy and independence. If the dominant fact in Armenia's life was the imminent, everpresent and overwhelming threat of Pan-Turkish attack, a permanent state of war was the only way to describe Armenia's condition. Democracy is, of course, the first victim of a state of war. The rejection of democracy was necessary also because the "protector" of Armenia, Russia, happened to have a non-democratic system. Armenia's governing elites—and increasingly those of the Armenian Diaspora—managed to nurture among the people a distrust of the ability of Armenians to adequately define their own interests, to make proper decisions regarding their own future, in short, to govern themselves.

Furthermore, the redefinition of Armenia's agenda—its needs and abilities—cannot be achieved without independence. Independence requires democracy. If Armenia's security as an independent state requires the normalization of relations with neighbors, the government of Armenia needs the mandate of the people, something which only democracy can grant. Such a change is certain to be resisted by extreme nationalists and fellow travellers, such as old-guard communists. Those uncomfortable with democracy have not been reluctant to argue against independence by raising the question of Armenia's lack of economic self-sufficiency—as if there are many countries in the world that are self-sufficient—if not the specter of Pan-Turanism, or both.

Many critics of the government's new thinking continue to insist on the need for some kind of union with Russia. Of course, the movement does not rule out any possibility, as long it is negotiated between sovereign states. Yet somehow continuing what was seems to be the obsession of those who, for whatever reason, have invested so much wisdom and energy rationalizing that which was created in 1920 and which allowed the people of Armenia to be abstracted, that which the people of Armenia have now rejected.

The sense of normalcy which the movement seeks to return to Armenian history requires both independence and democracy. For a nation that defined itself primarily as a victim and adopted survival as the ultimate goal, independence and democracy constituted dangerous ideals, luxuries at best.

Democracy is needed for rational discourse, for people to think and deliberate freely on their own agenda and priorities and to take responsibility for their decisions. It is not coincidental that the power that has made independence impossible has also decreed democracy undesirable. Both denials are motivated by the need to deny the right to think and imagine in a sovereign manner. The fear of Pan-Turkism and the specter of another genocide are the vehicles through which the denial of sovereign thinking and sovereignty are internalized and appear as Armenian interests rather than the interests of the imperial center and of those whose legitimacy depends on their connection with that center.

Finally, the strategy of the movement has also considered the possibility that independence may be forced upon Armenians—as it was in 1918—in the case of a collapse of the Soviet Union, seen as the most likely development. It would be a mistake for Armenia not to be ready for such an eventuality and to be manipulated by being drawn into a civil war not of its making.

For the first time in twentieth century Armenian political thought, independence and democracy seem to have evolved as pragmatic needs rather than abstract ideals in the Armenian national movement. In late nineteenth century Armenian political thinking—the national revolutionary movement—reform oriented goals were to a considerable extent formulated as Western inspired ideologies perceived as intermediaries between a backward Armenian nation and Western civilization. A remote republic within a closed empire, Armenia produced a movement within which contemporary Western concepts and terminologies appear as afterthoughts rather than determinants. These distinctions suggest a pragmatism, practicality, and flexibility that has in fact distinguished the course adopted by the ANM compared to national movements in other Soviet republics.

Armenia did have the advantage of a strong "opposition-in-exile"—the national party that had been instrumental in the formation of the first republic, 1918-1920, and that had kept the idea of independence alive—the Dashnaktsutiune. It is true that by the 1950s, for the Dashnaktsutiune, independence had become an anti-Soviet tool and, subsequently, a slogan useful in community politics and cultural identity. Especially within the last few years, the Dashnaktsutiune had abstracted the idea of statehood from its people and made possible the relegation of the ideas of independence and democracy in Armenia to the category of useful myths. The Dashnaktsutiune probably succumbed to the need of diasporans to feel comfortable with their choice of material comfort in the diaspora and preservation of a political-cultural identity in Armenia. Nonetheless, the torch had been passed on, so to speak, to an indigenous movement and a new leadership. Furthermore, even at the height of its power during the pre-World War I years, the Dashnaktsutiune did not relinquish totally the strategy of reliance on a "third force." This tendency was emphasized by its diasporization and was sanctified during the Cold War.

The new leadership of Armenian proposes to base the republic's security on a realistic understanding of its needs and resources, the appreciation of its strategic interests and possibilities, a strong economy and democratic institutions, and a viable national defense. The new leaders, now the leaders of the republic, propose to develop relations with all neighbors of the republic and are ready to accept the principle of negotiation to resolve outstanding issues. That which would have been unthinkable a few years ago—relations with Turkey—now can be contemplated because of the popular mandate which the government enjoys.

Underlying these strategic considerations is a mandatory change in Armenians' political self-definition. Just as it is necessary to free oneself from the psychology of the victim, Armenians must see themselves—and, by extension, their neighbors—as citizens of nation-states aiming at social and economic development rather than as representatives of ideologies, religions, and empires.

There must also be a change in political behavior. Armenia cannot afford to turn any issue into a "do or die" test. Building the future must be seen as a series of processes, not a legally or morally defined right or principle. While Armenia's change of policy and strategy does not guarantee a corresponding behavior within its neighbors, particularly within those whose internal processes have not as yet given their governments the same mandate to look for alternative strategies of negotiation and compromise. But, at the least, Armenia's politics will not exacerbate the situation and may possibly make a difference significant enough to avoid disastrous developments. That is better than the certainty of manipulation of relations, of pogroms and civil strife, by the imperial center, to justify its ultimate interest: the survival of the empire.

Armenia must address those issues which it can reasonably hope to resolve. The current leaders of Armenia find territorial demands from Turkey or Azerbaijan impossible to achieve. For them, the question of Mountainous Karabagh is a matter of human rights and national self-determination for the majority Armenian population of the region. The absence of Armenians, for whatever reasons, from other historically Armenian lands such as the six provinces in Eastern Turkey and Nakhichevan, present another problem. Their union with Armenia requires resources which Armenians simply do not have. The movement rejects, therefore, the formula most commonly promoted by the Dashnaktsutiune, "Territorial unity first, independence later," counterproductive for both goals—territorial unity and nation-building. A strategy of "demands," ostensibly to be fulfilled on the basis of international law or with the help of Russian arms is regarded by the movement as having little to do with reality. If Russia was interested in seeing a bigger Armenia, goes the argument, it could have done so with Karabagh and Nakhichevan. Ultimately, would argue the movement leaders, national goals and strategies cannot be abstracted from the people they are supposed to serve and from the realities of the situation.

The strength of the Karabagh Committee and the Armenian National Movement has been based on three factors. First, the ability of its leaders to present a coherent critique of the existing order without being ideological, negative, or vindictive; secondly, the ability to create credibility, to replenish the moral basis of political legitimacy after seventy years of destruction of the concept of politics and authority; thirdly, the ability to appeal to the masses' ability to think and judge, rather than to their emotions, by sharing with them not only their conclusions and decisions but also the process of argumentation, the logic underlying their policies and strategies.

A new strategy is often as problematic as the old. Will the new leaders of Armenia be able to translate their vision into a strategy and the strategy into programs? Will Armenia's neighbors reassess their own past behavior and current positions and respond positively to an opportunity to achieve real peace and security in the region? Can the redefined nation-state succeed where the ideological empire failed? Can democracy provide what ideologies could not?

The old strategy of survival for all concerned in the region has failed and, even if it could be reimposed by force, can not possibly inspire hope for a better world.

The stakes are so high and failure so expensive that for Armenians and Armenia, for peoples and governments in the region, there seems to be no choice but to reassess radically the bases of past relations—domestic, regional, and international—and seek answers to the real problems of real people.

Document One

RAFAEL ISHKHANIAN

The Law of Excluding the Third Force

This article is a critique of Armenian dependence on foreign forces—the "third force"—to achieve national liberation and survival. A historian by training and author of numerous publications, Rafael Ishkhanian argues that the strategy of reliance on Western, European, Russian or other governments has failed to resolve any aspect of the Armenian Question; on the contrary, such a strategy has had tragic consequences for the Armenian people. The lesson of history, asserts Ishkhanian, is to adopt a strategy that relies on Armenians' strength and resources, not those of other powers.

Ishkhanian's reassessment of the Armenian experience of the last three centuries is thus nothing less than a radical critique of Armenian historiography and politics. Ishkhanian is not the first to preach self-reliance. A comparison with a 1987 text written by Khajak Ter Grigorian (See Appendix B1) indicates that the same conclusion was reached by others within and outside Armenia. What makes this piece significant is that Ishkhanian is ready to take the argument to its logical conclusion and apply it to the present. In the context of Armenia's national movement, the logic leads to a redefinition of national interests and Armenia's relations with neighbors. In fact, as subsequent selections will show, we are looking at the redefinition of Armenia.

The article was written after the release from prison of the members of the Karabagh Committee, when it had become obvious that the regime was bankrupt politically as well as ideologically, and a thorough reassessment of the scope and strategy of the movement was under way. This text is a translation of the Armenian text as published in Haratch *(October 18, 19, 20, and 21/22, 1989), the Paris-based Armenian daily newspaper.*

I think man's main purpose in life is to achieve perfection. To go from bad to good; to change toward the perfect. I also think the same should be true for a nation, particularly for the Armenian nation: To realize the mistakes of our past, to make fewer mistakes in the future.

They say that the last words Stepan Zoryan[1] uttered before his death were his assessment of his people: "primitive nation."

Let us admit that a significant segment of our people and its leaders are politically naive. For example, to curse at Muslims and especially at Turks, to talk much about the Armenian Genocide, and to remind others constantly of the brutality of the Turks are all regarded as expressions of patriotism. Among the leaders of the past we consider those who cursed Turks and killed Turks to be the most patriotic. Our most recent heroes are those who assassinated Turkish diplomats in European cities.[2] Of course, this thinking is not true of all Armenians; but it is the dominant mentality. It is a psychological pole the other end of which is Europhilia and Russophilia. In 1985 the [Communist] party secretary of [Yerevan State] University said so in so many words: "The patriotism of Armenians is the love of Russians and hatred of Turks."[3]

During our recent history many of our writers and poets would begin [their texts] by detailing the suffering caused by Turkey and end by cursing the Turk and praising the Russian . . . Why

---

[1] Stepan Zoryan (1889-1967) was a Soviet Armenian writer.

[2] Refers to a campaign of assassinations of Turkish diplomats and officials, and armed attacks on Turkish targets by Armenian groups. The first incident occurred in 1973 when, on his own initiative, a survivor of the Genocide killed two Turkish consular officers in Santa Barbara, California. Armed attacks acquired a systematic and organized character with the emergence in 1975 of the Justice Commandos of the Armenian Genocide (JCAG) and the Armenian Secret Army for the Liberation of Armenia (ASALA). The campaign ended in 1983-1984.

[3] The statement summarizes aptly the attitude of those who define Armenian interests based on the need for an external power that must protect Armenians. This attitude is often shared by Western Armenians, who are likely to accept Russians as saviors based on a comparison with their experience with Turks. This was true before the Genocide in Ottoman Armenian provinces contiguous to the Russian Empire, and has been true, since, in the diaspora.

For that reason Armenian reformers and radicals advocating social, political, and economic change in Russian-dominated Armenia have often had trouble focusing attention on their agenda. The tone of the current political discourse in Armenia often reflects a reaction to a definition of liberation built on the premise that Russian Armenia's problems are relatively negligible. See Appendix C2 for another view of Russia's role in Armenian history.

do I bring in the writers? Because one of our tragedies has been that many of our political leaders were writers . . . and aesthetic literature has been taken as political program.[4] This, really, is an unfortunate confusion.

Zori Balayan,[5] who does not write in Armenian (all his Armenian publications are translations from Russian works) at every turn shouts "Death to the Turks." His book, entitled *Ojakh* (he apparently does not know that the word is Turkish) is dedicated to pleasing the Russians, to put the fear of Pan-Islam and Turks[6] in them, and to cursing the Azerbaijanis. "Fate has offered us to our neighbor in the north, to the great Russian people. Fate has also smiled at us since Eastern Armenia was saved by the Great October Revolution. Both peoples (Russians and Armenians) have had one common enemy. An enemy who lost its comfort the moment Eastern Armenia became part of Russia . . . "

Militantly anti-Turkish writings and publications have increased recently both in Armenia and in the diaspora. And

---

[4] This refers to the nineteenth century intelligentsia who produced the Armenian cultural Renaissance, followed by the political awakening. The tradition continued to some extent in the twentieth century.

[5] Zori Balayan is a Soviet Armenian writer. Born in Karabagh in 1935 and raised and educated in Russia (his father was in exile in Siberia), Balayan is a medical doctor turned writer and journalist. A naturalist and a staunch supporter of perestroika, Balayan first became active in Armenia's environmental movement. In 1987 he was instrumental in raising the question of Karabagh in Moscow, Armenia, and the West. In April 1988, when participation in demonstrations in support of Karabagh's request for self-determination had reached unprecedented proportions Balayan, along with poetess Sylva Kaputikian, was invited to Moscow to meet with Gorbachev. His influence in Armenia's national and democratic movement diminished as the leadership was institutionalized in the Karabagh Committee. Balayan's position on the role of Russia and Pan-Turkism goes a long way in explaining his loss of influence. See next note, and Appendices C1, C2, and C3.

[6] Pan-Islamism is the ideology of establishing a state that would include all Muslim peoples. Pan-Turkism or Pan-Turanism (Pan-Turanianism) is the ideology of establishing a united state that would include all peoples of Turkic origin. Both ideologies were used by the Young Turks during the First World War to first complement, then supplant the discredited basis of Turkish power and legitimacy, the Ottoman dynasty. The two ideologies, especially Pan-Turkism, have become associated with Armenian history as a cause of the Genocide of Armenians.

In Armenian political discourse Pan-Turkism has continued to inspire continued fear of the "Turk" and his goals, both in Armenia and the diaspora. The assumption here is that the only interest Turkey may possibly have with regard to Armenia is to destroy it and to exterminate its people.

Pan-Turkism has now become a major issue in the debate on Armenia's ability to exist and develop alongside Turkey. See Appendices C2 and C3.

the slogan "Turkey is our enemy and Russia is our permanent friend" is enmeshed in the brains of many Armenians.

It is obvious that our anti-Turkish psychological attitude is predicated on our knowledge of the power of Russia to the north. Turks and Azerbaijanis number approximately 65 million (if we include southern [Iranian] Azerbaijan) while Armenians throughout the world are six million, seven at most. According to statistics, Turkey's army is the strongest in non-Communist Europe, while we Armenians have no army. Turkey is an organized state, whereas we really have no state in the real sense of the word. When we wave our finger at Turkey, who do we have in mind as our support? Russia, of course, and the West to some extent.[7]

And this is our third force. The second force is our neighbors. [The Armenian people constitute the first force.]

When we look carefully at our political history during the last 300 years, we see that with one or two exceptions it was always based on reliance on the third force. That which we call today the Armenian liberation movement was based on reliance on the third force. When developing liberation plans, the main role has been assigned to the third force: the West and Russia.

As far back as the sixteenth century, Catholicos Mikayel sent Abgar Tokhatetsi to Italy.[8] Tokhatetsi conducted negotiations with the Doge of Venice and the Pope with the hope that Rome or Venice would save "Holy Zion" (Armenia) from "the infidels." Rome proposed that Armenians accept Catholicism. Abgar and his son accepted and promised that Armenians in general, too, would accede to the request. Of course, neither Rome nor Venice provided any support to Armenia. Why should they, particularly when they did not have the means to do so?

---

[7] The search for a savior or protector goes as far back in Armenian history as the thirteenth century when a weakened Armenian kingdom in Cilicia (northeastern corner of the Mediterranean), threatened by its neighbors, assigned that role to European states sponsoring the Crusades. Armenians laboring to liberate Armenia continued in that tradition. The emerging Russian Empire, physically closer to Armenia, also had more objective reasons to occupy Armenia. It became, therefore, a more integral part of the strategic thinking. See, among others, Ashot Hovannisian, *Hay-rus orientatsiayi dsagman khndire* [The question of the origins of the Russian orientation of Armenians] (Echmiadsin, 1921). Ashot Hovannisian (1887-1972) dominated Soviet Armenian historiography until his death, and in some respects, even after.

[8] This is the first of a series of such missions. Catholicos (spiritual head of the Armenian Apostolic Church) Mikayel Sebastatsi sponsored this mission in 1562. Efforts at liberation during the sixteenth and seventeenth centuries were mainly related to Eastern Armenia, then under Safawid-Persian rule, and had little to do with Western Armenia under Ottoman dominion.

Abgar's "liberation" mission was a childish undertaking, [based on] political ignorance.

But of course the most typical of such demarches was that of Israel Ori (1659-1711.)[9] In Germany, he convinced the head of a small principality (Pfalz) to lead his army to Armenia, to make war against Persia and Turkey, to liberate Armenia and restore the Armenian kingdom. Thus, starting from the banks of the Rhine river, the German prince with his army (in fact regiment) was supposed to cross half of Europe, Russia, and the Caucasus, reach the frontier of Persia, make war against it, win, restore Armenia's kingdom, and return to Germany. This most glorified instance of reliance on the third force was as ridiculous as that. And there are today historians who consider the hallucinating Ori a great political operative.[10]

When he realized that the prince of Pfalz was not delivering on his promise, Ori started to kowtow to Russia's tsar, Peter I. Here too, Ori made an appeal to Russia to destroy Turkey and Persia and to restore the Armenian kingdom. Obviously, Peter I did not need Ori or someone like him to undertake such an operation. Russia had its own interests and plans of conquest. The time was not ripe yet to vanquish the South Caucasus and Armenia and it was not Ori's appeal that was going to make Peter change his plans. The only consequence of Ori's activities was that he took his two sons to Petersburg, gave them a Russian education, and they became Russians.

One wonders about Ori, and not just about his naiveté. Why would Russia make war and shed blood to restore the Armenian kingdom?

I have read (I don't know whether it is true or not) that the diary of Peter I has an entry that expresses the view that Armenians should be exterminated by the hands of Muslims. Is it not possible that Ori himself may have indirectly inspired this idea in the Russian tsar? For a tsar who had undertaken the conquest of the world, the last thing he needed was some

---

[9] Ori was from the Karabagh region, most likely from nobility. His mission started as a member of a delegation led by Catholicos Hagop Jughayetsi in 1677. He is considered the first to adopt the "Russian orientation."

[10] Beginning with Ashot Hovannisian (See note 7), historians both in Soviet Armenian and in the diaspora, have glorified Ori for his dedication and the "wisdom" of adopting a "Russian" orientation that was to withstand the passage of time and regimes.

obstructionist Armenian kingdom.[11] Peter wanted the East for himself, not for Armenians or others.

Ori's initiative was the beginning of the "Russian orientation" of Armenians—more specifically, the adoption of Russia as the third force in Armenian political life. Western Europe and, generally speaking, the West remained, of course, part of Armenians' visualization of the third force. Russia, nonetheless, was the main power assigned that role. This role was so developed [by the end of the nineteenth century] that Grigor Ardsruni wrote, "We Armenians, politically speaking, are Russians."[12]

Davit Bek was contemporary to Ori.[13] Davit Bek appears as someone politically mature for his time. He concluded alliances with Georgia and Persia but did not rely on them as the third force. Davit Bek's activities are, in general, exceptional and worthy of closer attention.

In the 1780s, Armenian political activists in India, particu-

---

[11] Successive Russian governments have been careful not to lose sight of the fundamental reason for being in Armenia and the Caucasus, i.e. to maintain an empire. That central authorities wanted an Armenia without Armenians is arguable. One can be more certain regarding the kind of Armenian politics they could tolerate in Armenia. In 1783-1784 Archbishop Arghutian of Moscow offered the Russian court a draft treaty inspired by the "enlightened" Armenians of India according to which Russia would liberate Eastern Armenia from the Persians and an Armenian republic, endowed with a democratic constitution, and with manufacturing as the lifeline of its economy, would be created. The leaders of feudal Russia spurned the offer. After the conquest of Eastern Armenia in 1828, Armenian leaders who had supported Russian advances found themselves exiled or neutralized as Russia, run by landed nobility, found more comfort in the political support of the largely non-Armenian and conservative landowners of the Transcaucasus. In time the hereditary rights of the latter were reconfirmed. Despite Russia's antagonism with the Ottoman Empire, a reactionary Russian government cooperated with Turkish authorities in apprehending Armenian revolutionaries fighting the Ottoman regime, considering them "dangerous revolutionaries" not just for Ottoman Turkey.

The antagonism of central authorities toward the democratic forces in Armenia during the past two years and their support for communist-governed Azerbaijan, in the question of Karabagh, are part of the same logic.

[12] Grigor Ardsruni (1845-1892) was founder and editor of the first Armenian daily newspaper in the Russian Empire, *Mshak*, published in Tbilisi. Ardsruni articulated eloquently the positions of the Caucasian Armenian bourgeoisie on matters of fidelity to the Russian throne and Russian expansion into the Ottoman Empire as a solution to the Armenian Question.

[13] Davit Bek (?-1728) became the military commander of Armenian forces in Karabagh/Sunik that revolted against Persian rule in 1720. He distinguished himself not only as a military strategist but also as a political thinker who could force the fragmented *Meliks* or princes of Karabagh to leave aside their petty squabbles and imagine themselves fighting for a national cause, at least for a while.

larly Shahamir Shahamirian,[14] were proposing Georgia as the third force in Armenian political life. But this was a very brief moment. Russia continued to dominate as the third force throughout. At the beginning of the last century, the Armenian prelate, Archbishop Hovsep Arghutian, was in the avant-garde of the Russian armies moving into the Caucasus. During the 1827-1828 Russo-Persian War Archbishop Nerses Ashtaraketsi assumed the same role. Armenian volunteer corps were organized at the time to help Russian advances, and since then every time Russia has had a war against a Muslim power, Armenian volunteers have been organized and attached to Russian armies. Nerses was so naive at first that he believed Russia would restore Armenian statehood. That hope was shared by many, including Kh. Abovian.[15] Once it wrested Eastern Armenia from Persia, Russia went through the formality of organizing it as an "Armenian province." This formality was disposed of within two years.[16] Russia also exiled Nerses. Noting that Russia was not willing to restore the Armenian kingdom, Nerses Ashtaraketsi courted Russia and was elected Catholicos, while Baskevich, the conqueror of Yerevan, was writing home with instructions on how to debilitate the Armenians.[17]

[14] A significant Armenian merchant class outside Armenia evolved in Iran following the forced migration of Armenians to the Isfahan region at the beginning of the seventeenth century. Soon the trading domain of these merchants expanded to India, Europe, and Asia. In the eighteenth century, their expansion was supported—and regulated—by the British, who found it easier to penetrate the Indian hinterland by using the politically harmless Armenians. At the end of the eighteenth century, when the British East India Company no longer needed Armenian intermediaries, community leaders in Madras and Calcutta became quite active in a search for a homeland inspired somewhat by nostalgia but, largely, by a need to find a safe haven for their threatened capital. Shahamirian, a businessman himself, authored two books and sponsored projects in pursuit of this goal. In addition to Georgia, their search led them to negotiations with Russia as well. See also note 12.

[15] Khachatur Abovian (1809-1848) is the author of the first modern novel, *Verk Hayastani* [Wounds of Armenia], in Eastern Armenian literature. Educated in Dorpat (Tartu), Estonia, Abovian first welcomed the Russian annexation of Eastern Armenia but was soon disappointed. He disappeared in 1848.

[16] The elimination of the "Armenian Province" as an administrative unit and the first phase in the redrawing of the provincial boundaries within Transcaucasia based on imperial interests—with tragic consequences until today—were completed by 1840.

[17] Ivan Feodorovich Baskevich (1782-1856), commander of Russia's Caucasian Corps, signed the Treaty of Turkmenchai in 1828 with Persia on behalf of Russia that made Eastern Armenia part of Russia. Baskevich also served as governor of Transcaucasia.

Abovian blessed "the hour when the Russian's blessed foot set into Armenia."

Article 16 of the 1878 San Stefano Treaty foresaw the intervention of the third force into the affairs of Turkey, ostensibly in the name of Armenians. Article 61 of the Treaty of Berlin was similar.[18] This article was the genesis of the Armenian Question. In essence, that was the intervention of the third force in the affairs of Turkey in the name of Armenians, an intervention which ended with the total depopulation of Western Armenia of its Armenian inhabitants.

The Armenian revolutionary parties also placed their hopes on the third force, Russia and Europe. Even their names were copied from the Russians. *Hunchak* was the Armenian for Herzen's *Kolokol*; Federation of Armenian Revolutionaries was the exact translation of Russia's *Soyuz ruskikh revoliutsionerof*.[19]

---

[18] Following the Ottoman defeat in the 1877-1878 Russo-Turkish War, the warring sides signed the Treaty of San Stefano (February 1878). Western Armenians, led by Patriarch Nerses Varjabedian, sought the victor's support to secure reforms in the Armenian or Eastern provinces of the Ottoman Empire. In Article 16 of that treaty the Ottoman government pledged to introduce such reforms to ensure that the Russian army leaves the region. The Treaty of San Stefano was challenged by the Great Powers, mainly Great Britain, as too accommodating to Russian interests. The Treaty was revised at the Conference of Berlin in July 1878, with the participation of the Great Powers. Article 16 was replaced by Article 61 of the Berlin Treaty. The new provision diluted the strength of the first, despite the desperate efforts of an Armenian delegation headed by former Patriarch and populist clergyman, Mkrtich Khrimian.

This "internationalization" of the Armenian Question, which brought Russia closer to the West—and to the Ottoman Empire—on the Armenian issue, became controversial within the Armenian community immediately. The very conservative and frightened upper classes were concerned that the Patriarch's diplomatic initiative at a time of Turkish losses would raise doubts on the loyalty of the "loyal *millet*" or community. Others were suspicious of Russia's motivation and ability to manipulate Armenians.

[19] The first of the Armenian political organizations, established in Van in 1885, came to be known as the "Armenakan;" but it never evolved into a full-fledged political party. The first to deserve the name is the Hunchakian Revolutionary Party (later the Social Democratic Hunchakian Party). It was founded at the end of 1887 in Europe. It was followed by the Federation of Armenian Revolutionaries (soon Armenian Revolutionary Federation (ARF) or Dashnaktsutiune) in 1890 in Tbilisi. Involved in guerrilla warfare before 1908 against the Ottoman Empire, the latter two became legal parties in Turkey following the 1908 Young Turk Revolution, along with a new party, the Ramgavar Sahmanadrakan (Democratic Constitutional) Party.

The Dashnaktsutiune, the most important of the three, played a major role in the establishment of the first republic of Armenia, 1918-1920. After the sovietization of Armenia, all three have been active in the diaspora only and have been involved largely in community organization and cultural activities. All

The main function of these parties was to organize a movement by armed groups and to invite the attention of Europe to Armenia when massacres occurred. In other words, their whole strategy was to invite in the third force.[20]

Here too the mentality of reliance on the third force expresses itself through immature actions: Occupation of the Ottoman Bank and threats of destroying it with bombs,[21] making bombs to assassinate the Sultan,[22] and such activities. Anything to invite the attention of the third force. The main purpose of the *fedayee* movement was that too.[23]

There were individuals, of course, who regarded anti-Turkish activities based on reliance on the third force destructive to Armenians. Ormanian was one of them. Our revolutionaries, in love with the third force, humiliated him and dragged him into the mud.[24] A. Isahakian[25] writes that Ghevond Alishan[26]

three are making efforts to develop followings in Armenia since the election of a democratic government there in 1990.

[20] While such an argument can be made, the strategy of Armenian political parties prior to 1920 is best characterized, in the opinion of the editor, by indecision. The political parties did make serious efforts to work through the constitutional system of the Ottoman Empire to bring changes, whenever any possibility or hope of success for such a strategy arose. More often than not, however, they relied on Western Powers to pressure the Ottoman government. This was as much a matter of strategy and the absence of options as of cultural self-definition.

[21] On August 24, 1896, a group of Dashnaktsakans (members of the Dashnaktsutiune) occupied a branch of the Ottoman Bank in Constantinople, an act considered the first recorded act of urban terrorism. The group threatened to blow up the building with its occupants (and contents) unless Western governments intervened to put an end to the massacres of Armenians in the Eastern provinces. Western diplomats made an informal pledge to look into the situation; the attackers were led out of the country; the massacres continued and spread to the capital.

[22] The plot to assassinate Sultan Abdul-Hamid II was conceived and planned by one of the founders of the Dashnaktsutiune, Kristapor Mikayelian. The attempt, on July 21, 1905, failed to kill the Sultan. Mikayelian himself had been killed earlier when experimenting with a time bomb in Bulgaria. See Appendix A2.

[23] It is possible to characterize the *fedayee* or guerrilla movement against the Ottoman Empire as a peasant rebellion, a mechanism to defend families and crops in a disintegrating rural economy; or, as a demonstration of Armenians' virility, therefore an assertion of the right to be taken seriously. It is correct to assert, nonetheless, that the organizers of the movement never made up their mind whether the ultimate purpose of the movement was to destabilize the empire sufficiently to necessitate Western intervention or, as was claimed on occasion, to function as a revolutionary force capable of overthrowing and replacing the regime. See also Document Five, note 14.

[24] Maghakia Ormanian (1841-1918) one of the more educated and conservative

too was against the use of the third force by Armenian revolutionaries, saying "We should not provoke the Mongolian blood of Turks." But these were just individuals dismissed by the majority as Turkophiles.

When the third force or any of its components failed to behave as we projected and used the Armenian question to their interests, we would become angry, we would curse Europe and Russia but would still continue to place our hopes on them.[27] We could not see an alternative way to liberate Armenia. We went so far as to cast Bulgaria in the role of the third force.[28]

The Dashnaktsutiune, realizing that there was no hope from the tsars, at one point became indignant with Russia and adopted an anti-tsarist and anti-Russian attitude, and made some attempts at befriending the Turks.[29] In 1914 it formally promised Turkey to remain neutral in case of a Russian-Turkish war.[30] But it was enough that canons started exploding on the

---

clergymen active in Western Armenian life. He was Patriarch of Armenians of Turkey from 1896 to 1908, when he was deposed by a crowd of angry Armenians following the Young Turk Revolution in 1908.

[25] Avetik Isahakian (1875-1957) was the dean of Soviet Armenian poets; he had studied in Europe before the Russian Revolution.

[26] A revered member of the Armenian Catholic Mekhitarist Congregation of Venice, Father Ghevond Alishan (1820-1901) was a philologist, historian, geographer, poet, and linguist who had a major impact on the nineteenth century Armenian cultural renaissance and political awakening.

[27] Moralization has played a major role in Armenian political discourse as long as Western Powers have failed to behave as Armenians expected them to, both before the First World War and since, especially in the diaspora.

[28] Refers to a special relationship between Armenian revolutionaries, especially the Dashnaktsutiune, and the Bulgarian government prior to the First World War. The relationship involved the opening of an Armenian military school, the participation of former guerrilla fighter Andranik (See note 38) in Bulgarian military operations against Ottoman Turkey and, in general, cooperation in anti-Ottoman propaganda.

[29] Anti-Russian feelings among the Dashnaktsakans and Hunchakians can be traced to the anti-tsarist activities of the Russian-Armenian born founders of both parties. Both parties participated actively in the Russian revolutionary movement of 1905. It is probably fair to assume, however, that had Russia been more supportive of the Armenian parties in their anti-Ottoman struggle, the Hunchakians and Dashnaktsakans may have been less inclined to be involved in anti-tsarist activities.

[30] In early 1914 the Young Turk government entered a secret alliance with Germany. The Turkish leaders informed the Dashnaktsutiune regarding their decision to enter the war on the side of Germany in the summer of 1914 when the Dashnaktsutiune was completing a World Congress in Erzerum. The Turkish delegation requested that the Dashnaktsutiune use its considerable resources on both sides of the Russo-Turkish border to help Turkey's forthcoming war effort

border for the ARF to join all of its forces with the Russian side.[31]

In the second half of 1914 Armenians were in a joyous mood. "Russia will win the war against a fatally weak Turkey, our arch enemy, and the Armenian Question will be resolved," was the song. Almost all Armenian intellectuals, including writers such as A. Shirvanzade[32] and H. Tumanian,[33] had joined the chorus.

There were intellectuals then too, who were against the formation of Armenian volunteer units in the Russian army. Aram Manukian[34] was one of them, accompanied by the leadership of the Dashnaktsutiune in Van. But their view was not shared. H. Kachaznuni[35] returned to Tbilisi from Van and communicated to

---

against Russia in return for the promise to establish an autonomous Armenia in Eastern Turkey after the war. The leaders of the Dashnaktsutiune urged the Turks not to enter the war, warning of the possibility of the total disintegration of the empire, to no avail. Party leaders refused the Turkish request, saying Armenians on each side of the border would have to serve the armies and strategy of the government under which they lived.

[31] While true for the organization in the Russian sector, this was not generally true for Ottoman Armenians. Even as the threat of Genocide loomed large, Armenian leaders continued to urge their youth to heed the Ottoman army calls for military duty. This made possible the massive and efficient extermination of large numbers of Armenian young men who could otherwise have joined local groups resisting the deportations and massacres. This general trend is hardly counterbalanced by the famous act of Armen Garo, a member of the Ottoman Parliament and of the Dashnaktsutiune, who left the Ottoman Empire to join the Russian side at the start of the war.

Ishkhanian's reference is specifically to the formation of volunteer army units attached to the Russian army and made up of Armenians, sponsored by the Dashnaktsutiune-led Armenian National Council in Tbilisi. See note 37.

Eventually many Western Armenians joined the volunteer units. The real question not adequately addressed in historiography is whether the Armenian volunteer units constituted a cause or an excuse for the deportations and massacres leading to the Genocide? It is possible that Ottoman Turkish policies left no doubt in the minds of some Armenians that their fate was sealed and participation in volunteer units was one form of resistance.

[32] Alexander Shirvanzade (1858-1935) is an Eastern Armenian playwright and author.

[33] Hovhanes Tumanian (1869-1923) is a major figure in Eastern Armenian literature and cultural history.

[34] Aram Manukian (1868-1919), a leading member of the Dashnaktsutiune, organized the defense of Van in 1915 and Yerevan in 1918. He is considered the founder of the Republic of Armenia in 1918.

[35] Hovhanes Kachaznuni (1868-1938), a leading member of the Dashnaktsutiune, became the first Prime Minister of independent Armenia. Kachaznuni broke ranks with his party in 1921. At the 1923 party conference in Vienna, Kachaznuni delivered a significant speech, subsequently published as *Dashnakt-*

the ARF Bureau[36] the position of the ARF leadership there against the formation of volunteer units. He also expressed his own position, which was strongly against such an undertaking. He ended up in a conflict with Doctor Zavriev,[37] who was a most devoted promoter of the third force strategy. But some time later Kachaznuni himself became an enthusiastic organizer of the volunteer units.

Our reliance on the third force reached its zenith during the First World War and our losses reached their zenith as well; we came very close to being exterminated completely.

This piece of Armenia [Eastern or Soviet Armenia] was saved by one person who, with farsightedness, ruled out reliance on the third force. He was able to keep this territory and created a new Armenian state without a third force. I am speaking, of course, about Aram Manukian.

When we look back now, we realize that since 1915 and perhaps earlier, two opposing directions were evolving. One consisted of reliance on the third force, in this case Russia, and of seeing Turkey as the eternal enemy. It is possible to call this direction the Zavriev-Andranik[38] approach. (We should not forget that Andranik refused to recognize the Armenian republic, which was created without Russia's help.) The other approach was based on the principle of ruling out reliance on the third force and developing a dialogue with neighbors based on an accurate accounting of one's resources. It is possible to call this the Aramian approach. The latter approach did not preclude external assistance if such was available. Aram

---

sutiune anelik chuni aylevs [The Dashnaktsutiune has nothing more to do], in which he argued that the party had contributed what it could to history and it was time for it to dissolve itself.

[36] The Bureau or Buro is the highest executive body of the Dashnaktsutiune. See Appendix B2.

[37] Hagop Zavriev (?-1920) was a Russian speaking Armenian physicist active in the Dashnaktsutiune. He had strong ties with Russian diplomacy. In the Fall of 1917, Zavriev was appointed Vice Governor of Western Armenia, during the brief period of Russian occupation of the region.

[38] Andranik (Ozanian, General Andranik, "Brave Andranik," "Andranik Pasha;" 1865-1927) is the most famous of the Armenian guerrilla fighters, although not necessarily the most important. He represented the emerging new image of the Armenian who could fight. In addition to his service in the Dashnaktsutiune guerrilla force, Andranik served in the Bulgarian army in its war against the Ottoman Empire in 1911 and commanded one of the Armenian volunteer units attached to the Russian army during the First World War. His relations with the Republic were never solid, as he was made ineffective by his ever-changing reliance on British, then Russian strategy, and lack of trust in the ability of the republic to survive on its own.

[Manukian] was not even opposed to getting help from Bolshevik Russia; but he refused to rely on any external force. He always made plans considering the national strength, saying "What you see is what you get." One of his famous statements on the subject deserves to be quoted: "No one is interested enough in Armenians to send tangible assistance. On the contrary, there is a conspiratorial attitude. We are alone and we must rely only on our own forces."

Among Armenians then and now, the dominant approach has been the Zavriev-Andranik line. In May 1918, Turkey demanded that the three nationalities in the Transcaucasus secede from Russia and declare themselves independent republics. The Georgians and the Azerbaijanis were in favor. Armenians, including the Dashnaktsutiune, were resolutely against it. In the Seym[39] Georgians and Azerbaijanis voted for independence, Armenians voted against it. This is a well-known fact. Why did they vote against independence? Because Armenians could not imagine themselves separate from the third force, or Russia; reliance on the third force had become part of the Armenians' instincts. This was true for the Bureau of the Dashnaktsutiune as well as the National Council,[40] both sitting in Tbilisi. They distrusted the national strength so much that they did not even reside in Armenia. One of those representing this mentality was General Nazarbekian who, when commanding the Russian army, was constantly ordering attacks, but when given a command in the Armenian army, decreed nothing but retreat. Had decisions been taken by the likes of the National Council of Tbilisi, Andranik and Nazarbekian,[41] the Turks would have occupied Yerevan as well, and that would have meant the end of Armenia.

But in Yerevan there already was an independent Armenian state headed by Aram Manukian. Contrary to the decisions of the National Council and Nazarbekian, Manukian organized brilliantly the defense of the new Armenian state already in

---

[39] The parliament of the federated Caucasian republics of Armenia, Azerbaijan, and Georgia prior to their full independence in May 1918.

[40] A Council made up of representatives of Armenian organizations and prominent personalities in Transcaucasia. The Council was organized with the encouragement of the Russian government and acted as a quasi-government for major Armenian undertakings, such as the organization of volunteer units and care for refugees of the deportations and massacres. The Council was dominated by the Dashnaktsutiune.

[41] Tovmas Nazarbekian (1855-1928), a general in the Russian army, served the Armenian republic following the Russian Revolution and the collapse of the Russian army.

existence, based solely on Armenian forces, and then entered into negotiations with the Turks. And the Armenians, always being massacred and always on the run, were able to win finally. For the first time, the Turkish army retreated because of the Armenian army. (But Armenians have forgotten the victor and glorify the defeated.) Thus, the greatest victory of the Armenians was achieved without the third force. This [victory] is our lesson. When Georgia in Tbilisi and Azerbaijan in Baku declared independence respectively on May 26 and May 27 [1918], the Armenian National Council was forced to cut its umbilical cord from the third force (Russia) and, although outside the boundaries of Armenia, it declared in Tbilisi the independence of Armenia. That was May 28 [1918]. Members of the Dashnaktsutiune, perhaps not all of them, later understood that May 28 had a fateful importance for Armenian life. Although the Armenian state existed before that day, it was approved on that day. It was particularly important because on that day, Armenian leaders liberated themselves from their instinctive dependence on the third force and felt themselves alone in facing our neighbors, especially Turkey.

Simon Vratsian writes in his memoirs that in February 1917, during the [Russian] revolution, Armenians were not ready for independence.[42] The Georgians were fully ready, Azerbaijanis partially, Armenians not at all. We were also not ready for independence in late 1917 or early 1918 when the Russian army was deserting the Caucasian front and running away from Armenia. The gentlemen who had catered to the whims of Caucasian Viceroy Vorontsov-Dashkov and had organized the Armenian volunteer movement were confused: The Russians were leaving, what are we supposed to do?

Before that turn of events, in 1915, Western Armenians were slaughtered in proximity of the Russian army and the volunteers. One or two Kurds would massacre a whole Armenian village. The powerful Russian army and aroused Armenian volunteer units were singing Russian hymns and enjoying barbecues. They moved not a finger to help the Armenian population that was being raped and slaughtered. Where were you, Armenian *fedayees*? Where were you, Brave Andranik? Where were you

---

[42] A leading member of the Dashnaktsutiune, Simon Vratsian (1882-1969) was involved in the organization of the volunteer forces, despite his opposition to the policy. During the period of the first republic, 1918-1920, Vratsian served as editor of the party newspaper, minister of labor, and prime minister. He published his memoirs in six volumes under the title *Keanki ughinerov* [Along the paths of life] (Cairo and Beirut, 1955-1967).

heroic volunteers? There was no Turkish army in those parts [easternmost parts of the Ottoman Empire]; the Turkish army had been destroyed near Sarighamish in January 1915.[43] Had Armenian units marched into those areas many would have been saved. They did not move because they could not visualize themselves acting without the third force. The tsarist army itself was waiting to see that Armenia was left without Armenians, as had been the plan.

Where were you, Doctor Zavriev, originator of the Armenian volunteer units, you who crowed against the Turks and provoked them. Zavriev was the most important figure among Russian-speaking members of the Dashnaktsutiune who believed in the third force, the likes of whom we can find amongst us today.

The Armenian National Council finally was kind enough to [leave Tbilisi and] come to Yerevan after May 28.[44] The Dashnaktsutiune became a state party. And it seemed it began to understand the redeeming value of ruling out the third force. But that lasted only until the signing of the Treaty of Sevres.[45]

[43] Refers to the Third Ottoman Army led by Young Turk Minister and one of the ruling triumvirate, Enver Pasha. The army was decimated due to bad planning and the harsh winter near Sarighamish on the border with Russia. Enver is supposed to have praised the bravery and dedication of Armenian soldiers in his army, while the general Armenian population of the region became the scapegoat for his defeat.

[44] Tbilisi, the regional capital, was more a city to their liking. Yerevan had very few of the amenities of the financial and industrial center which Tbilisi had become with the help of the Armenian bourgeoisie. Living in Yerevan was a problem for many. The group included Boghos Nubar Pasha, the Paris-based Armenian diplomat whose family had served the British in Egypt and who claimed to be the best candidate for Minister President of the new republic. The leaders of the Republic were ready to consider the option, if Boghos Nubar was ready to move to Armenia. Boghos Nubar declined to do so.

This is a continuing problem in diaspora-Armenia relations as diaspora parties now make claims on the loyalty of the citizens of Armenia. The current government has supported the right of diaspora parties to function in Armenia and compete for power as long as the leaderships of the parties are in Armenia and do not constitute external forces. The same condition has been set for Armenia's Communist Party which has been politically and organizationally dependent on the Party of the USSR.

[45] The Treaty between the victorious allies and the defeated Ottoman Empire, signed on August 10, 1920. Armenia was a signatory of the Sevres Treaty as the "little ally." The Treaty recognized Armenia's independence and left the decision on boundaries to the arbitration of President Woodrow Wilson of the United States.

The Sevres Treaty, superseded by the Treaty of Lausanne (1923, See note 52), has been an important basis of arguments until now supporting Armenian claims on Eastern Turkey.

In the summer of 1920 there was an opportunity to enter into relations with the Kemalists. Kemal[46] would have welcomed it, since he was in a bind and was willing to cede Kars and a portion of *vilayet* of Van to Armenia.[47] But the policy of reliance on the third force had resurfaced among Armenian leaders. Prime Minister of Armenia, the doctor Hamo Ohanjanian,[48] was waving the Treaty of Sevres and demanding from Turkey an Armenia with borders defined by that treaty. This time it was the West that was supposed to help. This expectation continued, despite the British statement that the British fleet could not climb Mount Ararat,[49] despite French preoccupation with its own affairs (preparing the treacherous surrender of Cilicia to Turkey).[50] Armenian leaders continued to place their hopes on these states, unwilling to realize that the Treaty of Sevres had, for Armenians, no more value than a piece of paper.

Aram [Manukian] was no longer there. [Mustafa] Kemal, not finding an echo in Armenia to his initiative, allied with Bolshevik Russia; the two divided Armenia between themselves and the Republic of Armenia died.[51] The Western countries did

[46] Mustafa Kemal or Kemal Ataturk (1881-1938), leader of the Turkish nationalist army that fought against the dismemberment of Turkey, overthrew the Ottoman government set up after the end of the First World War, and founded the modern Republic of Turkey.

[47] This assertion is open to question.

[48] A leader of the Dashnaktsutiune (1873-1947), Hamo Ohanjanian served the Republic of Armenia as a prime minister.

[49] Statement attributed to British Prime Minister Benjamin Disraeli (1804-1881), justifying the British position of support for the Ottoman Empire and "abandonment" of Armenians at the Congress of Berlin.

[50] Sizable Armenian communities still lived in Cilicia following the First World War. The area had been occupied by the French with the help of the Armenian Legion. At first, as part of France's Legion of the Orient, the Armenian Legion was composed of Western Armenian volunteers eager to fight Turkey following the depopulation of Armenia. In calling Armenians to help occupy Cilicia beginning in 1916, the French led Armenians to believe that Cilicia would be turned over to an Armenian administration. The French and the Armenian Legion did occupy Cilicia by the end of the First World War. The Armenian Legion was dissolved. In 1921 the region was turned over to the Turkish nationalist army, however, and Cilician Armenians were left to their own devices. A declaration of independence in Adana had no chance of success. Few Armenians were left in Cilicia by the end of 1922.

[51] Armenia was Sovietized on December 2, 1921, although the Soviets celebrated November 29.

The current boundaries of Armenia with Turkey were delineated in the Treaty of Alexandrapol (later Leninakan, now Gumayri) between Turkey and Armenia at the same time as Armenia was being sovietized. The Alexandrapol Treaty's boundary provisions, by which Armenia ceded much territory, were confirmed by

not lift a finger. At the conference of Lausanne, the Armenian delegation was like a raped woman who had come to complain.[52] It had no protectors. This was another example of the consequence of the policy of relying on the third force.

Defeat is a bad word, no one likes it. When I say that our liberation movement was defeated, my friends don't like it. I don't like it either. But it is a fact. We were defeated.

The aim of the Armenian national liberation movement, begun in the mid nineteenth century, was to liberate Western Armenia, more precisely to introduce reforms in the six eastern [Ottoman] *vilayet*s, to establish Armenian autonomy. That aim was not realized. In addition, Western Armenia (historical Meds Hayk) or the Armenian-populated six *vilayet*s were deprived fully of their Armenian population. Cilicia, Pokr Hayk [central Anatolia][53] and other areas within Turkey were depopulated of their Armenian inhabitants as well. And Surmalu and Kars, which had previously been under Russia, became part of Turkey[54] and lost their Armenian population.

This is an ignominious defeat. And the main reason for that defeat is our reliance on the third force. Had we ruled out any kind of third force and had we developed our plans on the basis of our own resources and moved accordingly, we would have avoided this kind of ignominious defeat.

Our historians, whose main task during the last 70 years has been to cover up, remain silent in the face of this defeat. And it is very harmful not to inform the nation about its own defeat and not to identify the causes of that defeat. One should tell the truth so that the mistakes are not repeated. A nation that does not learn the lessons of its own history has no future.

Incidentally, our other critical victory, in Zangezur in 1920-

---

the Treaty of Kars and Treaty of Moscow signed in 1921 between Soviet Russia (on behalf of Soviet Armenia) and Turkey.

Ishkhanian's interpretation may be based on an oversimplification. Armenian reactions and attitudes constitute only one set of factors, albeit an important one, that determine Soviet-Turkish relations.

[52] Armenia was not a participant in the negotiations that led to the signing of the Treaty of Lausanne in 1923. That treaty replaced the Treaty of Sevres (See note 45). Other than indirectly through articles dealing with the religious and cultural rights of minorities in Turkey, the Treaty of Lausanne has no reference to Armenia or Armenians.

[53] Central Anatolia was, in part, within the boundaries of historic Armenia.

[54] Regions in the northeast of Turkey and part of historic Armenia which were under Ottoman rule until 1878 and Russian rule between 1878 and 1914. These came under Armenian dominion during the republic but reverted back to Turkish control in 1920. See note 51.

1921 and led by Njdeh, was also without the help of a third force.[55] We have always lost when we have relied on a third force.

Our historians and both communist and non-communist political leaders have always inspired the thought that [Armenia] cannot survive without Russia, that Russia is the savior of Armenia, etc. In other words, they have always argued that we cannot live without the third force.

This line of argument reinforced the slavishness that has developed among stateless Armenians since 600 A.D., at least for the last 900 years, since the fall of Ani.[56] The extent of russification among Armenians is due to the reinforcement of this slavishness. The majority of the intelligentsia in Armenia today is Russian-speaking and writes in Russian. Tens of thousands of Armenian families living in Armenia are Russian-speaking. And the number of Armenian children attending Russian schools is close to 100,000. Over 90% of the internal administration of Armenia is done in Russian. I am not even talking about [Armenians in] the North Caucasus, Rostov and Russia, Armenians who did not end up in those places because of any massacre or exile.[57] Armenia today has been russified tangibly and is moving toward full russification. If we continue on this path, we will be finished. And this is another consequence of our reliance on the third force.

The concept of and tendency to rely on the third force debilitates the internal strength of Armenians, turns them into sycophants, kills their spirit of resistance, and destroys their will to survive.

Now [these sycophants] are throwing at us the scarecrows of Pan-Islamism and Pan-Turkism, so that we Armenians attach ourselves more tightly to the Russian carriage. The knights of the third force are telling us that, without Russia, Pan-Islamism and Pan-Turkism will swallow us. At this point I do not wish to develop this argument further, or talk about the substantial issues of Pan-Islamism and Pan-Turkism, or demon-

---

[55] Garegin Njdeh (1888-1955) was a military commander in the service of the army of the republic credited with victories against the Bolsheviks and Azerbaijan.

[56] The fall of Ani in 1045 A.D. marks the end of Armenian dynastic control of historic Armenia. Ani was the capital of Armenia under the Bagratuni dynasty.

[57] Armenia's population is approximately 3.6 million, including Artsakh's approximately 140,000. There are still over 400,000 Armenians living within the boundaries of Georgia, very few left in Azerbaijan, and approximately 500,000 in Russia and other parts of the USSR.

strate that those of our leaders who are constantly frightening our people with such arguments are, to say the least, ignorant.

The primary purpose of peoples who do not have statehood is to obtain or restore statehood, meaning independence. This purpose applies to Armenians as well. If we do not have this purpose, we are condemned to oblivion. But I think we have it, to some extent.

But the birth of an independent Armenia depends on the favorable international circumstances and on the degree to which the Armenian people is ready for it. I said that from 1917 to May 28, 1918, we were not ready for it. We are not ready now, because we have made our existence conditional on the protection of a third force.

Toward the end of 1917, when the Russian armies were leaving the Caucasus, Zavriev and the Zavrievians were pleading with Russia not to leave, since they could not imagine Armenia without Russia. But no one listened to them. Is it not possible, though, that events now will progress in a similar direction, that the Russian army will leave Armenia? No one can exclude that possibility. Even if our knights of the third force such as Z. Balayan,[58] H. Simonian,[59] S. Kaputikian,[60] S. Poghos-ian[61] and others at that moment come to their knees and plead with them "Don't leave, brothers," no one will listen to them. No third force has ever acted on a plea by Armenians and no third force will do so now. Each [power] has its own interests and plans. We invented the view that Russians saved us. When Russians hear that statement they are surprised. "When have we saved you? Why should we have saved you?" Europe, too, can say nice things about Armenians but it will not help militarily; it has never done so and it never will (if it has no interest of its own).

Thus, if Russia leaves Armenia, the three million Armenians living on a 20,000 square kilometer territory will find themselves facing our five neighbors (Azerbaijanis, Turks, Iranians, Georgians, and Kurds) who number in the tens of millions.

---

[58] See note 5.

[59] A contemporary Soviet Armenian writer.

[60] Sylva Kaputikian is a contemporary poetess in Armenia, one of the group of intellectuals who were instrumental in raising the question of Karabagh early in 1988 and leading mass demonstrations. Like Balayan, Kaputikian too lost her position within the emerging leadership. See note 5.

[61] Stepan Poghosian (b. 1931), a contemporary historian of modern Armenian history. Poghosian was elected first secretary of Armenia's Communist Party in December 1990.

The law of ruling out the third force requires that at present we imagine ourselves facing those five neighbors alone. Once we start thinking that thought, much will change. We will immediately begin to seek ways of finding resolutions to our conflicts instead of showering [our neighbors] with sterile curses. And we will begin preparing for statehood. We will be ready.

I repeat. Ruling out the third force does not mean excluding allies. An ally is someone with whom our interests coincide, even if for a brief moment. And we will have allies only when we have our own strength. But one does not rely on allies, one does not make plans on the power of an ally. An ally only assists. The more we become a vassal of Russia the less it respects us. Russia will respect us when we end our slavishness.

But we, as a nation, in our mind, instinctively, have become incapable of ruling out the third force. We rely on it, we curse our neighbors, and we develop a strategy based on the strength of the third force. This attitude is shared by unofficial organizations in Armenia as well as Armenian national organizations [in the diaspora].

Let us take the Dashnaktsutiune. The full range of its activities are conducted on the basis of reliance on the third force. In an interview I read, one of its leaders, Mr. Marukhian,[62] has stated that the creditor of the Armenian territories is the USSR, meaning Russia (although I should repeat that Russia has never had the intention, nor does it have now, of returning Armenian territories to Armenia.) It is the same Dashnaktsutiune which is knocking at the doors of another third force, Western powers and the UN, to have them recognize the Armenian Genocide.[63]

---

[62] Hrair Marukhian has been a member of the Bureau of the Dashnaktsutiune since the 1960s and its chairman since 1972. Marukhian's position adequately represents the position of the Dashnaktsutiune party, since there has been an increasing concentration of power in his hands during the past decade, particularly since the process of change has been accelerated in Armenia. The trend is the same for many other organizations in the Diaspora, although very few have the impact of the Dashnaktsutiune. For Marukhian's views, See Appendix B2.

[63] The strongest and best organized of the three diaspora parties, the Dashnaktsutiune was the most adamant opponent of Soviet Armenia and the party that continued to believe in independence, to the point of internalizing anticommunist cold war ideology during the 1950s and 1960s. Anti-Dashnak rhetoric, in turn, was a necessary ritual for any government or official in Armenia.

In the seventies, the Dashnaktsutiune refocused on Turkey as the main enemy and on Genocide recognition as the immediate concern.

The Dashnaktsutiune has followed a course antagonistic to the national democratic movement and to the present government. It has joined the other parties

I was discussing the issue with a leader of the Dashnaktsutiune. He said:

—No, it is impossible to have a dialogue with Turkey. Turkey pursues only one aim with regard to Armenians, to annihilate us.

—Then why is independent and free Armenia your goal as stated in the party program if you do not believe it is possible for a free Armenia to exist as a neighbor of Turkey?

—Some third force must help us, such as Russia.

—But on what basis do you believe that Russia will tolerate a free Armenia and will help it?

—We have no other solution. Also, our first task must be the return of our territories.

—But everything changes in this world. Once Romans were here, they left; there were Byzantines, they left. Is it not conceivable that Russia will some day leave the Transcaucasus? What will we do then?

—We will find another sponsor.

—Who do you have in mind?

There was no answer. I continued:

—And on what basis do you believe Russia or some other power will take our territories from Turkey and give it to us? Who taught you that? Ask Russia and see what it says.

—It's all the same. We cannot survive, we cannot achieve anything without the help of some major power.

—If we cannot live on this land as a sovereign state having Turkey as a neighbor, then we should all be ready to leave our homeland with the Russian army. That is what you are preaching. I believe we must think about how to preserve Armenia in this given environment, not on how to destroy it.

The position of the "Hay Tad"[64] group in Armenia is approximately the same as that of the Dashnaktsutiune. Even more: If the Dashnaktsutiune still considers the Armenian language, the problem of schools, and the education of new generations important, "Hay Tad" considers language, schools, education, the use of Armenian by Armenians, in other words, the

---

in assuming that Armenia needs Russia as a protector, that independence can or should be attained only following the reunification of Western Armenian territories to present day Armenia, and that Pan-Turkism is the greatest threat to Armenia. See Appendices A1, B2, and C1.

[64] The term means "Armenian Cause." The political arm of the Dashnaktsutiune uses the same Armenian words for its "Armenian National Committee."

Armenia's Hay Tad group is led by Hovik Vassilian. It is not considered a trustworthy group as some suspect it of close ties with state agencies.

question of our cultural survival unimportant, witness their periodical. [Hay Tad members] are all concerned about "our land." It appears they believe that by screaming "our lands, our lands," someone, perhaps Russia or the West, will give Armenia those lands. They are not thinking that while they are demanding those lands and slighting Armenian language and culture, Armenia and the Armenian people may be assimilated; what would the territories unite to if there was no Armenia left?

Moreover, "Hay Tad" is looking for new enemies of the Armenian people. This time it has put its finger on Jews. It is fighting on three fronts: against Pan-Turkism, Pan-Islamism, and Zionism, always relying, of course, on Russia.[65] And although Russia has said and is still saying that it has no intention of fighting Pan-Turkism and Pan-Islamism and it is making efforts to have a rapprochement with Israel, our "Hay Tad" is still waging the same battle, "fighting" on three fronts. It is now appropriate to repeat the words of Jivani, "Come to your senses."[66]

Our Ramgavars[67] and Hunchakians[68] too are relying on the

---

[65] A strand of anti-Semitism has penetrated the discourse in Armenia probably in imitation of Russian nationalists.

[66] Ashugh Jivani, Armenian minstrel (1846-1909).

[67] Ramgavar Azatakan Kusaktsutiun (Armenian Democratic Party), formerly Ramgavar Sahmanadrakan Kusaktsutiun (Armenian Constitutional Party), one of the three parties that continued to function in the diaspora following the Genocide in Western Armenia and the Sovietization of the Republic in Eastern Armenia. The party has a program with a Western liberal orientation; it was organized in 1908 after the Young Turk Revolution as an alternative to the Hunchakians and Dashnaktsutiune which were socialist oriented and did not shun armed struggle. The Ramgavars were not able to develop roots in Eastern Armenia, although they did want to participate in the governance of the Republic since they claimed to represent Western Armenians.

The Ramgavar Party accepted the Sovietization of Armenia as a pragmatic reality and adopted a policy of support of Soviet authorities as a way of supporting Armenia. The Ramgavars argued that Armenia had no chance of becoming independent any time soon and, considering the Turkish threat, the Russian presence was a necessity for its survival.

In line with their logic that it is their duty to support Armenia no matter who governs it, the Ramgavars have declared their support for the new government. They have, however, disagreed with the government's declared interest in developing neighborly relations with Turkey.

[68] The Social Democratic Hunchakian Party, the oldest Armenian party, declared in 1923 that with Sovietization, the Armenian Question had been resolved satisfactorily. In line with their "Marxist" orientation, the Hunchakians declared their ideological support for the Soviet state as well.

The Hunchakian position further complicated the paradoxes in Armenian politics, since the Hunchakian Party was the only one of the three to have adopted independence as a goal at the time of their founding in 1887. Armenia, then, meant Ottoman Armenia, of course, and independence was the last resort against third force, in this case Russia. They too are incapable of visualizing any kind of Armenia without Russia. It has now been 50-60 years that their whole politics is based on the mentality of full devotion to the idea of Russian protection.

The third force is also relied upon by our Yerevan independentists, the "Self-Determination Group" and the group that seceded from them.[69] The leader [of the Self-Determination Group] is Paruyr Hayrikian, who is very dear to me.[70] Hayrikian has made a speech at the European Parliament on the independence of Armenia, having hopes on that Parliament. He sends letters and tapes to Armenia demanding that independence be declared here, that armed forces from the UN and the European Parliament be invited; these are the third forces on which the Self-Determination Group relies.[71]

Our independentists who rely on the West as the third force are antagonistic toward Russia. I think that to declare enmity toward Russia or the West is as senseless as relying on them . . .

The independentists are disappointed in Russia and are cursing it. But why did you place your hopes on them [to begin with]? Who told you that Russia is the savior of the Armenians? Russia itself has never said that. This, my fellow citizens, is your invention. It is you who have placed your hopes on those powers and are now disillusioned. We must be fair. It has now been 300 years that Russia's leaders have been telling us, "When you and the Muslims are in conflict don't expect us to defend you." And their behavior is in conformity with that position. Callously we return [to the same belief] and hope that Russia will be on our side against our Muslim neighbors. And it

---

an Ottoman state that offered little chance of generating reform. The Hunchakians are the weakest of the three diasporan parties.

[69] The group was organized in 1965 as the "United Armenian Party." Its program has changed over time, but independence remains central to it. Currently, it functions as the National Self-Determination Group. The organization publishes the *Hayrenik* [Fatherland] monthly and has support groups in the Diaspora.

[70] Paruyr Hayrikian, the founder and leader of the organization, served 17 years in Soviet prisons for his political views and activities. Hayrikian was exiled from the USSR in 1989 and resumed his activities in Europe and the United States. In November 1990 Hayrikian was allowed by the Soviet authorities to return to Armenia and claim his seat in the new Parliament to which he had been elected in absentia.

[71] Hayrikian receives his main support in the West from groups and sources closely identified with conservative and reactionary causes such as US Senator Jesse Helms and newspapers such as *The Wall Street Journal* for whom Hayrikian's stand on relations with Turkey combined with his virulent anticommunism are of special interest.

has now been 300 years that we have been advising the Russians that the Muslims are the bad guys, that the Muslims are Russia's enemy, that we Armenians are the good guys. We have written so many books and articles to convince the Russians that they should defend us, without ever getting any results. The Russian state has much experience and understands perfectly its interests. It is not up to us Armenians, who have no state and no [such] experience, to teach them. "Kemal deceived Lenin," "Azerbaijanis have bribed the Kremlin," "The wives of politburo members are Tatars and Turks, that is why the politburo members do not defend us," are the types of irrational, immature explanations offered by many Armenians.

No, dear ones, Lenin knew perfectly well who Kemal was; from the point of view of the interests of the state he was leading, Lenin pursued a perfectly logical strategy by helping Kemal in any way he could; we were the duped ones who in 1920 did not find some understanding with Kemal and lost Kars. You can also rest assured that Azerbaijan has not bribed the Kremlin. The Kremlin has its own line and it is not at all friendly toward Armenians. It is also a major act of stupidity to link Russia's refusal to side with the Armenians to Turkish women or in-laws. That mentality too has a history of 300 years . . .

When Nikolai Ryzhkov was in Armenia, he met with the Armenian intelligentsia. Speaking at that meeting, Z. Balayan repeated the same old story: Muslims, Azerbaijanis, and Turks were the bad guys; Armenians were the good guys; therefore Russians should protect us. Mr. Ryzhkov admonished him: "Put an end to that. It is not you who will teach us how to behave or tell us who is good and who is bad. We know very well what we are supposed to do." And he was right. But Z. Balayan did not learn his lesson. In his speech at the Armenian Supreme Soviet in 1989, pronounced in Russian, Balayan repeated his appeal to the Russians and informed them that the Turks were the bad guys, that we were good, and that there was the threat of Pan-Turanism against which they should protect us.[72] Still no result. One should be ashamed of the situation. How long can one go on without learning the obvious. The Russians are refusing to accept your definition of their interests, but you insist on teaching them. It also does not make sense to be enemies with Russia. Not to rely on Russia, not to make plans based on its power does not at all mean to be enemies with Russia. Let us be friends, but let us not rely on them, be so fully devoted to them,

---

[72] Nikolai Ryzhkov, Prime Minister of the USSR. See Appendix C2.

believe so much that they are our saviors. Let us re-Armenianize Armenia, let us be our own nation. And you know what? Russia will then begin to respect us.

Many Armenians are angry at M. Gorbachev because he is not giving Artsakh to Armenia. But my dear Armenians, who among his predecessors gave us Artsakh? Lenin? Stalin? Malenkov? Khrushchev? Brezhnev? Who? No one. This systematic refusal indicates that removing Artsakh from Azerbaijani jurisdiction and annexing it to Armenia is against Russian interests. Why are you angry at Gorbachev himself? He went so far as to allow you to make demands on behalf of free Artsakh, to form an "Artsakh Committee." His predecessors did not even allow that. We must finally understand that no leader of Russia can go against the interests of Russia.

The European Parliament. That body recognized the fact of the Armenian Genocide.[73] And many Armenians were overjoyed that the European Parliament recognized that Turks slaughtered and raped us, that they killed and burned us, and that they buried us alive . . . The European Parliament has its own calculations, and for the umpteenth time, it used the Armenian Question as small change. The members of the European Common Market do not want to see underdeveloped Turkey join the market and so they brought in the Armenian Genocide and told Turkey "You have slaughtered Armenians . . . therefore there is no room for you in the Common Market." They are exploiting our greatest tragedy and we are laughing flippantly.[74]

Generally speaking, it is meaningless to seek recognition of the Genocide by different countries or the UN. Let us assume that all the countries and the UN recognized that we have been slaughtered. What then? Our naive Armenians tell us, "The return of our lands would follow." My dear fellows, what does the recognition of Genocide have to do with the return of the

---

[73] On June 18, 1987.

[74] Reasons for the rejection of Turkey's membership include anti-Muslim prejudices and racism, and the fear of current members with economies that have a strong agricultural sector such as Spain, Portugal, and Greece that Turkey may be too strong a competitor. Armenian organizations have generally actively opposed Turkey's membership in the European Common Market based on the arguments that such a step would further strengthen Turkey, make it more respectable in the international community and, generally, be an insult to those nations that have been harmed by Ottoman-Turkish policies. The Armenian government's developing thinking on Turkey may give more credence to the opposite but unorthodox view among some Armenians that Turkey's membership in the European Common Market may be a strong incentive to remain within the bounds of acceptable behavior with regard to its neighbors.

lands? For example, the genocide of the American Indians is recognized by the UN. Why aren't the white Americans leaving America and returning those lands to the American Indians? How long will we remain naive? Moreover, have you thought to whom the territories will be returned? To Russia (i.e.the USSR)? Is Russia short of land? Russia (the USSR) has formally declared that it has no territorial demands from Turkey. And, finally, if Russia does take territory from Turkey, why do you think it will give it to the Armenian SSR? If Russia was the kind of power that gave to Armenia, it would have given what it has in its pocket, Artsakh and Nakhichevan[75].

But I have digressed from the issue of our independentists. They apparently believe that independence will come by shouting "independence." It appears to many of them that they invented the idea and the word independence. As if no one before them, from Aram Nahabed[76] to Aram Manukian, no Armenian political figure had ever sought independence. By shouting "in-de-pen-dence" in the streets they are anointing themselves prime minister and provisional government of Armenia. Just as children play homemakers, so are our independentists playing independence. None of that has anything to do with the real independence of Armenia.

My dear independentists, independence will not be achieved by the unending repetition of that word. How did we achieve independence in 1918? It will come the same way in the future. We must prepare for it so as not to be surprised by it as we were in 1918. First the Armenian nation must attain sovereignty and independence psychologically, mentally, morally. That is why we must eradicate the idea of relying on a third force and we must establish relations with our five neighbors. We must be able to assure our people that it can survive without relying on xa third force. And it is necessary—and very important today—that we re-Armenianize today's russifying Armenia, considering that many of the independentists cannot even sign their names

---

[75] Nakhichevan is a historically Armenian region to the southwest of today's Armenia. In 1923, over 50% of its population was still Armenian. Like Mountainous Karabagh, it was awarded to Soviet Azerbaijan, although it is not contiguous to that republic. Currently less than 2% of its population is Armenian. The Nakhichevan example of demographic changes under government pressure, leading to loss of effective control of the land, and the need to avoid its fate add an important dimension to the struggle of Karabagh Armenians for self-determination.

[76] A legendary king of Armenia whose story may have some foundation in history.

in Armenian, that others don't know Armenian in general and write in Russian only and are shouting independence.

The latter gather in front of the Matenadaran,[77] in full view of Mesrop Mashtots's statue[78] and shout, "It is wrong to focus on the problems of speaking or writing in Armenian or Armenian education; what we need is independence. Once we have independence all other problems will be resolved automatically." Very well, gentlemen, in case that independence is delayed by 10, 50 or 60 years, can we while screaming independence, wait till Armenia is russified? I asked one independentist,

—Why aren't you signing in Armenian?

—Why is that important? It's independence that counts. I will start signing in Armenian when we have independence.

—Then should we all sign in Russian until independence?

—Why not.

That is the measure of the brain of our independentists. I ask,

—My neighbor's son will be starting school this year. Should he attend Armenian or Russian school?

—What's the significance of that? What matters is independence.

These people do not understand that Armenia's independence begins with writing in Armenian, speaking Armenian, and providing Armenian children with an Armenian education. What kind of an Armenian are you, when you are not liberated from the yoke of the non-Armenian. No one needs an independence whose consequence would be to teach Armenian children to think in other languages.

He who in the name of independence is creating obstacles to having all Armenian children learn in Armenian schools and Armenianizing 100% all internal communications of the government is the real enemy of our independence.

Our most genuine, our greatest independentist was Mesrop Mashtots who, at the moment of the disintegration of the Armenian state, gave us the Armenian alphabet, language and

---

[77] Main repository of ancient Armenian manuscripts, the second most popular site for public meetings, since the beginning of the movement in 1988. The first was the Opera Square, renamed Freedom and Independence Square.

[78] Armenian scholar credited with the invention of the Armenian alphabet around 400 A.D. Mashtots and the alphabet constitute the most important symbols of cultural identity and regeneration. In 1989, when the agenda of the movement had become most encompassing, school children were seen demonstrating in the streets of Yerevan chanting the alphabet as if it was the most revolutionary song.

literature, gave us Armenian schools and, as a result, although without political independence, we kept our moral and cultural sovereignty. But today's independentists, standing in front of Mashtots's statue, are rejecting Mashtots . . .

Finally, our path to becoming a sovereign and independent nation will become barren if we forget our Christian faith, which is being denied the majority of our nation today.[79] If we try to do everything without relying on our Maker, we will fail. Our nation has been kept and will be kept by God, if we rely on Him. He has never turned away from us; it is us who have done so and fallen onto bad days. We need a return to Christianity like we need the air. Let us rely not so much on a third force but on God and on the strength we can develop.

And thus, our independentists are relying fully, whether they want to or not, on the UN, the European Parliament, etc., as a third force. The nation can only suffer from such a course.

The newly created party of National Independence seems to proceed more cautiously although, it seems to me, it has not been able to rid its mind of the thought of a third force.

The Artsakh Committee [Karabagh Committee] also started its work by relying on the third force. Who did it appeal to in order to achieve the reunification of Artsakh and Armenia? Moscow. That means it was hoping that this third force would resolve the conflict between Azerbaijan and Armenia in our favor. I believe it was in February of 1988 that there was a meeting at the cultural workers' home where the well known among Armenians met: S. Kaputikian, Z. Balayan, S. Khanzatian,[80] S. Sargsian,[81] members of the Artsakh Committee, etc. Everyone was quite convinced that Moscow (the third force) would return Artsakh in the spirit of perestroika. I told those gathered, "During the last 300 years, no one has ever given us an inch of territory. On what basis do you believe that [Russia]

---

[79] Armenians are proud of being the first Christian nation and consider the Church a national institution that must be respected and guarded at all times. Therefore the critical attitude regarding Armenian historical institutions is rarely applied to the Armenian Church, as it is seen as a venerable institution that unites all Armenians.

Nonetheless, over the years the Church has lost much of its appeal as a spiritual home; and the role played by Catholicos Vazgen I during the last two turbulent years did not help matters in the eyes of the supporters of the movement. Nonetheless, there is a wave of religiosity and spiritualism in Armenia today which is not necessarily articulated through the established Church.

[80] Sero Khanzatian (b. 1915) is a popular writer of historic novels.

[81] Sos Sargsian (b. 1929) is a well known actor who has assumed a visible political role in support of the reunification of Karabagh.

will do so now? I can't see any reason." I was left alone in a chorus that relied on the third force. For some time after that the Artsakh Committee believed that the third force would act in our favor. I have proposed that on the question of Artsakh the Committee enter into direct negotiations with Azerbaijan. They tell me, "Azerbaijan will not relinquish." "But," I tell them, "isn't it true that Moscow will not give either?" Negotiating with Baku will at least lighten this extremely painful enmity, and then it is possible that better conditions can be created for the Armenians of Artsakh.

It has been 68 years, since 1921, that we have been sending appeals, petitions, historic documents, etc., to Moscow, demanding the just solution to the problem, i.e. the reunification of Artsakh with the Armenian SSR. All these papers would probably fill a truck.[82] Nonetheless, we received nothing.

The slogan pronounced by the Artsakh Committee, "We have no permanent friends, we have no permanent enemies," was a step toward moving away from reliance on the third force, a sign of political maturity. The Committee's statement on Pan-Turanism at the Supreme Soviet is similarly a move in the right direction.[83] But at present, the Committee's current activities still do not indicate a tendency toward real sovereignty. The Committee, too, is indifferent toward the problems of our language, toward the issue of the Armenianization of Armenia. The care of the language and Armenianization are yardsticks by which will be measured the direction and goals of any Armenian organization.

I should add that next to the language-education issue, the most critical one is the cleaning up of the polluted environment of Armenia.

I ask myself: If in fact Russia does at some point withdraw its armies from the Transcaucasus, what will be our situation—a nation still relying on the third force and surrounded by Muslims? We will be shocked again, because we are not ready for it. It is clear that the Moscow-oriented bigwigs will run to Moscow. And those of us who remain on this 29,000 square kilometers? It seems to me there is no organization today that can provide the leadership for this people and undertake serious negotiations with our neighbors. That organization, that force must be created now. We must begin negotiations and develop the idea of

---

[82] See Gerard J. Libaridian, ed., *The Karabagh File*, (Cambridge: Zoryan Institute, 1988).

[83] See Appendix C3.

surviving on our own, now.

I am convinced that we can survive in this environment if we move not with our emotions and a sense of vengeance but with reason . . . In this case God will help us. And if we survive, become strong, and do good deeds, our lands will be reunited too.

But if we refuse to act with logic, if we become prisoners of our emotions, of the call of revenge, this piece of land too will be taken and we will be lost as a nation.

For 300 years, we have relied on the third force and we have lost for 300 years. We kept this piece of land because we did not rely on the third force, we ruled it out. We must learn a lesson from Aram Manukian.

And thus, the only correct path we can take, and the problem that has the highest priority, is the moral and intellectual sovereignty and independence of our people, based on the law of ruling out a third force.

No one will resolve the Armenian Question. We Armenians are the only ones who can resolve it. And the Armenian Question can be resolved only when we accept and apply the law of exclusion of the third force.

Document Two

Four Questions to Vazgen Manukian

This interview, which consists of five questions, touches upon the difference that has evolved between the thinking of the Armenian National Movement, now the government of Armenia, and the position traditionally taken by Armenian political groups on a critical issue: What is the relationship between two major national concerns, unity of historic Armenia and independence? Must one precede or have priority over the other? What are the possibilities of attaining either goal? What are the implications of each answer? Manukian answers these questions based on historical experience and current political calculations. In a sense, he continues Ishkhanian's argument and comes closer to deriving a political program from it. The interview is also significant for the qualifications it places on the democracy which the movement expects to foster in Armenia while building a new state.

Vazgen Manukian is a mathematician by training. Until recently, he taught at Yerevan State University. Manukian was one of the members of the Karabagh Committee, and of the Executive Committee of the Armenian National Movement. In August 1990, he was designated Prime Minister of Armenia.

The full text of the interview with Manukian was first published in Hayk *(number 4-5, 1990), the official organ of the Armenian National Movement and, subsequently, in* Haratch, *March 24-25, 1990. This text of the interview is based on the first translation that appeared in the* Armenian Update *(March 1990), published by Zoryan Institute, Cambridge, Massachusetts.*

Q uestion: In your opinion what goals should the Armenian nation seek? In what ways have the movement's two years contributed to the realization of these goals?

Our people have two national political goals: the reestablishment of independent statehood and the territorial question, i.e. the return of those lands that have been forcefully taken from us. The end result of the realization of these two goals will be that Armenia will occupy its rightful position among other civilized nations.

These two political goals have been, on occasion, brought together in a single formula, the creation of an independent and united Armenia.[1] It is necessary to note, however, that these two propositions, at some point, are mutually exclusive. Each one of these problems, independence and territorial unity, requires its own strategy and different sets of friends and enemies. It is therefore not possible to resolve both problems at the same time.

I would like to discuss the question of Karabagh as a separate question. Today's Armenian republic and Karabagh are the only two territories from historic Armenia that are still inhabited by Armenians. The problem of the reunification of these two is now posed.

[. . .] We must examine and determine which of the two goals must have priority: The reestablishment of independent statehood or the return of occupied territories? Which of the two is feasible today?

Before we go too far in that analysis, we should note that in order to resolve the territorial problem we must have independent statehood. No one will donate a piece of land to us, no one will conquer it for us. No one will do for us what we must do for ourselves. The last two years have reconfirmed, again, that simple political truth. Our people must concentrate, therefore, on the question of the reestablishment of our independent statehood. Without independent statehood it is impossible to resolve territorial questions, whether one is thinking of a political or a military strategy.

It is not incidental that even the Karabagh question, which is not a simple territorial problem, brought our people to the idea of independence, wittingly or unwittingly. In dealing with the issue of the reunification of Karabagh, every radical step we were taking brought us closer to the behavior of an independent state. Only then were we able to reach some results.

---

[1] In 1919, when it was the party in power, the Dashnaktsutiune proclaimed Free, United, and Independent Armenia as its goal. That has remained to date, officially, the formula summarizing that party's aims. In recent years, however, independence has been relegated into the misty future and the unification of Armenia is seen as preceding independence.

The question has arisen today: Is it possible to reestablish independent statehood? Here [those who answer in the negative] see two obstacles. First, Armenia today is a land occupied by Russia, and history shows that states do not willingly give up occupied territory. It is logical to assume, it is argued, that Russia will prevent the reestablishment of our independent statehood. But the political situation in Russia today is such that the solution of that problem does not seem so remote. Having remained less developed than other countries, Russia is trying to resolve two mutually exclusive problems simultaneously: On the one hand, to strengthen Russia economically, politically, scientifically, and culturally; on the other hand, to preserve the empire. To preserve the empire, it must use force; to develop the country it must cede some liberties to the people. Development is possible only when people are free. Freedom and democracy have a tendency to encourage centrifugal forces. This effect is particularly visible in the economic arena, where disintegration is proceeding at an accelerating pace. In the process of resolving these two mutually exclusive problems, wittingly or unwittingly, it is probable that Russia will have to resign to the idea of keeping some republics within its boundaries, just as it had to resign to the loss of control of eastern European countries. In the present situation, therefore, we may have reason to believe that if we pursue the right path, the general situation of the USSR will provide us with an opportunity to achieve independence.

Others point out the second obstacle. Once we achieve independence, [they argue], we will have to face powerful Turkey, whose purpose it is to destroy Armenia and join up with Azerbaijan, with which it shares to some extent a common religion and ethnic background. Let me respond first to those who use this argument against independence.

First, we must understand that the Russian army is here to protect the interests of the empire and not to defend Armenians. The USSR is an empire in the process of disintegration; its interests require that sooner or later its armies leave the area. Whether we like or it not, we must face that problem.

With regard to the unification of Turkey and Azerbaijan: No two nations of the same ethnic background have ever unified in the twentieth century. On the contrary, each ethnic unit has tried to achieve its own statehood. For that reason, one should not be concerned about that particular prospect; rather, if it ever got there, the problem would be a Turkish conquest of Azerbaijan by going through Armenia. Azerbaijan, too, wants to be independent just as any other nation. In Turkey there are, of course, people who talk of unification with Azerbaijan. There are political circles who are pursuing that question and are arguing that such a unification would be in the interest of Turkey. However, the weight of those who give such a definition to Turkey's interests is not so significant.[2] The dominant concern in Turkey is more like that which characterizes our period: The development of the country's economy, production, science, and culture.

Now, it is difficult to guess which of those approaches will become dominant if the political situation changes. That is also the case for all countries. No country has any guarantee that its neighbor will not attack it. That is why each country develops its own strategy and creates armed forces appropriate to the situation. When Armenia obtained independence in 1918, it was in a very serious situation, but it was able to withstand the Turkish attack. Those peoples who wish only to benefit from the advantages of independence but are afraid of independence are condemned to oblivion, and the world is no poorer for it.

During the two-year life of the [national] movement, tens of thousands of Armenians became deeply conscious of these simple truths and concluded that in order to resolve our problems we must forgo our Russian orientation. This, of course, is not at all the same as being anti-Russian. Our people understood that in the pursuit of our political goals we can rely only on our own forces without, of course, negating the idea of having allies. We do look for allies, but not sponsors. We must realize that we can obtain independence only when we have correct, non-antagonistic relations with all our neighbors.

Question: I noted that in discussing our occupied lands you avoided using the term "demands."[3] Was this incidental?

No it was not. The term "demand" borders on the ridiculous. It serves to cover up a poor strategy: To appeal to the world to demand justice. I prefer a policy which, rather than pleading justice at every corner, conquers it based on cold calculations, wise strategizing, and force.

[2] A small party advocating Pan-Turkism received only 1% of the vote during Turkey's last elections.

[3] The term "demands" is the common characterization of items on the national agenda as formulated by diasporan parties. Originally coined when the parties were functioning in the Ottoman Empire, the term has survived and continues to serve diasporan psychology.

Question: What kind of political tendencies do you see currently in Armenia?

The arena is full of political organizations. New armies and fronts are born every day, many of them made up of three or four people.[4] I know of an organization that is made up of one person.

The times when it was dangerous to deal with politics and when two or three organizations filled the arena are gone. For some, politics is a profitable preoccupation. Each organization writes its program and defines goals quickly and tries to win a place in the political arena. It is all quite confusing. But all of this is only on the surface. On the surface we also see [the consequences of] human pretensions, confrontations that are incomprehensible to many, and fraudulent appeals for unity.

Deep down there is a powerful and irreconcilable struggle between two positions, only two. I described the first in responding to your first question.

What is the second position? Underlying that second position is the following visualization of the problem: We are a small, Christian nation surrounded by an ocean of Muslims hostile to us. Consequently the only way we can survive and avoid physical extermination is by accepting the protection of some Christian power. And, naturally, our eyes are set on Russia.

What is the price for that orientation? To give up the goal of independence. Or, by proving a commonality of interest, induce Russia to use its force to occupy our territories and, only then, pose the question of our independence. The inducement would be the threat which Pan-Turkism poses to the Russian Empire as well as to Armenia. Such logic forces us into exaggerations. And it allows all those who have a problem with Turkey to use us for their interests.

That policy was used brilliantly early in the century and in return we were massacred.

The adherents of this strategy are now proposing that we use it one more time. First of all, it should be clear that it is not we who must explain to Russia where its interests are and who its

---

[4] The Armenian National Movement itself represents some forty groups. During the past two years there were attempts at organizing competing fronts, one claiming over 30 organizations. Of course not all are, strictly speaking, political. But, under the circumstances, the proliferating groups seldom distinguish between political and, for example, cultural activities. Moreover, within a society that was totalitarian until recently, there is very little that does not have a strong political component.

enemies are. That is ridiculous. Secondly, what does common interest mean? If we, and the Russians, and the Kurds all want Van,[5] that does not mean that our interests are now coinciding, since each wants it for itself. If for a moment we forget that Russia is a disintegrating empire and argue that it has the capability of conquering Van, then rest assured that Russia will not turn Van over to Armenians just as it did not hand over Karabagh and Nakhichevan[6] to Armenians. Awarding Karabagh and Nakhichevan to Azerbaijan was not a policy peculiar to the Bolsheviks nor the consequence of Stalin's hatred of Armenians. That award was not made because leaders in Moscow were corrupt or thickheaded. That was the way Russia defined its imperial interests, and if we refuse to understand this point, we are condemned to repeat the same mistakes, always paying with the lives of our compatriots and with whatever remains of the lands left to us by our ancestors.

By following this policy line, by serving Russia's interests, we are only provoking our neighbors, including the Christian Georgians; we are gaining nothing. And we are denying our nation the opportunity to deal with the problem politically and militarily—by relying on its own strength to prevent and defend against possible tragedies. Those who are pushing this policy and being promoted by Moscow, such as the Balayans[7] and the Galoyans,[8] will depart with the Russian armies; our people will remain and suffer the thorny fruits of their shortsighted strategy.

When the Ottoman Empire was disintegrating, nations that were struggling for their independence—such as the Serbians and Bulgarians—were saved, and they reestablished their statehood. The Armenians, who strove for reforms by relying on the benevolent support of Western powers or tried to replace the protection of Ottomans with that of Russians, were massacred [. . .]

To avoid physical extermination, to enable us to defend ourselves, to achieve national goals, to have self-respect, and to be

---

[5] City of historic importance to Armenians, in southeastern Turkey, currently inhabited by a large number of Kurds.

[6] See Document One, note 75.

[7] Zori Balayan. See Document One, note 5.

[8] Once a vice-president of the Armenian Academy of Sciences, Galoyan served as chief of the ideological sector of the Central Committee of Armenia's Communist Party during the past two years. He was reelected to his old post in December 1990.

respected by others, there is only one path—the path to independence.

Question: What are the main problems the ANM proposes to address in the next few months?

The most important question is the forthcoming election to the Armenian Supreme Soviet. For the first time, the population of Artsakh will be participating as well. The ANM will do everything to ensure that the campaign is conducted in the freest of conditions so that people can elect their representatives.[9]

What expectations do we have of our future parliament, our Supreme Soviet? We often compare the current situation with that which evolved earlier in the century. There are, of course, many similarities. But here is one major distinction. The big difference between now and 1917 is that we now have a state. It is true, that state is not independent, it is in a semi-slavish condition [. . .] What can I say, there is much that we can complain about concerning our republic. Nonetheless, there are state mechanisms that can be used to pursue our national goals. The Supreme Soviet elections and a good parliament give us the possibility to make that mechanism work somehow, to free ourselves from our slavishness, and to proceed step by step toward sovereignty and independence.[10] The current political situation enables us to think that these are problems that can be resolved. These are the prospects if, of course, events proceed normally.

But, just as in eastern Europe events suddenly and unexpectedly accelerated, so too the situation can change suddenly in the Transcaucasus. It is necessary therefore to have organized self-defense and to be ready for all eventualities. This important problem must be resolved parallel to the preparations for the elections. What we are proposing is simple: To be ready for war but try to prevent it with a political strategy. Incidentally, we should observe that our historical experience and recent turn of events indicate that nothing helps peace more than a realization by the enemy, by his experience, that his every strike will be followed with a powerful counterstrike.

Question: What is your position on democracy?

---

[9] The elections produced an AMN-led majority.
[10] See Document Seven.

Mankind has produced different systems, different mechanisms of government. In the economic domain, [the most acceptable] is the market economy. All those who refused to adopt that economic system condemned their economies to destruction, and created obstacles in their countries for their development of science and production, such as we see in the communist countries.

Similarly, countries that were not governed democratically condemned their populations to backwardness and created deep social inequities and injustices. But there is no single way to define democratic governments. The Greeks, the Japanese, the Americans each have their own democracies. These coincide in the fundamentals and differ in details; they also change in time, adjusting to the particular problems people are facing. Accordingly, each democracy has its own boundaries that reflect traditions and mores, unwritten rules. In Japan, for example, democracy is limited by thousands of unwritten rules that determine citizens' lives.

Given our people's long history of statelessness, of being partitioned between different empires and the adjustment of different segments to the customs and mentalities of different empires, we have lost much of the common unwritten rules. For that reason democracy on a grand scale can be deadly to our people; it can lead to atomization and it can cut off the precarious links of mutual responsibilities that tie us together. It is very important to us to revive our national traditions, religious traditions, and morality. The boundaries of our democracy will be determined by those factors. Otherwise we would constitute a mob, not a nation. Without having the pretension to define those boundaries, allow me to mention one of the relevant categories. The most important factor that binds us together and defines us is our language. When we lose the language, we stop being a nation. Our democracy then must allow us to ask that all Armenians speak Armenian and have all Armenian children attend Armenian schools. No Russian schools on the territory of Armenia. Some say it is not important what the language is, what matters is what is being said. That is a lie, a dangerous lie for our people. The first is as important as the second.

Document Three

HAMBARTSUM GALSTYAN
The Riga Meetings

These excerpts from an interview with Hambartsum Galstyan provide a glimpse of the thinking of the leadership of the national movement in dealing with Armenia's neighbors. Galstyan is speaking of the meetings held in February 1990 with representatives of the Azerbaijani Popular Front (APF) in Riga, Latvia. The discussions did not lead to a resolution of the conflict in Karabagh; the defeat of the APF in Azerbaijani elections in September 1990 made a follow-through even more difficult. Yet for the Armenian leadership, negotiations remain the most acceptable way to resolve conflicts with neighbors. As the first instance of the application of the new thinking, the Riga discussions were symptomatic of the reaction they would elicit from within Armenian political circles.

Hambartsum Galstyan was a participant in the Riga discussions. He is one of the first members of the Karabagh Committee and continues to serve on the Executive Committee of the Armenian National Movement. In December 1990 he was appointed mayor of Yerevan. He is a senior researcher at the Institute of History of the Armenian Academy of Sciences and specializes in ethnic issues of the Transcaucasus.

The interview was conducted by Haratch *and published in that newspaper on March 1, 1990. This translated text first appeared in the March 1990 issue of the* Armenian Update.

The press in the Armenian Diaspora, and the West in general, has often, intentionally or otherwise, described the Riga meetings as negotiations. These were not negotiations. The Baltic Council[1] invited the Armenian National Movement (ANM) and the Azerbaijani Popular Front (APF) to participate

---
[1] A council of cooperation and coordination composed of representatives of Latvia, Estonia, and Lithuania.

in political consultations.[2] The invitation did not exclude the possibility of direct meetings between the two organizations if the two sides had no objections [. . .] The ANM Executive approached the proposal seriously and decided that we should go. From purely tactical considerations, had we not accepted an invitation to such a meeting, which could in the future lead to negotiations, it would have been impossible for us to explain to the world why the Azerbaijanis wanted a political solution to the issue and we did not. This would have been viewed as exacerbating the situation.

[. . .] In substance, the ANM's position is a corollary to the incontestable truth that the Azerbaijanis and the Armenians have to live with each other in the region. And, in accordance with this truth [. . .] the escalation of tensions between the Azerbaijanis and Armenians in Karabagh should not be viewed as a unique event in the history of civilization [. . .] There have been moments in history where tensions between neighborly peoples have reached and surpassed the level of war. Invariably, meetings and negotiations have followed these wars [. . .] If, through such meetings as in Riga, we can save even one life without compromising our just cause, then it is immoral not to do so.

[. . .] Some curse us, saying that we had no right to come forward on behalf of the entire Armenian population. We did not do so; the invitation was very clear. It was addressed to the ANM and the APF. We came forward on our own behalf; we did not exceed our mandate [. . .] We are not a government and did not pretend to conduct negotiations on behalf of the government.

[. . .] The Baltic Council had an interest in these meetings. Bringing the conflicting sides around a minimal common denominator and repairing the confrontational relations between these two peoples would have given the Baltic Council great legitimacy in the eyes of the Soviet government [. . .] Also, it is no secret that the Baltic states, benefiting from rights guaranteed in the constitution, want to secede from the Union and are following the events in the Caucasus with grave concern. If the exacerbation of relations between the Armenians and the Azerbaijanis leads to large scale conflict, the central authorities will be forced to resort to mass suppression, which can extend to other parts of the Union. Such a precedent is very dangerous to the Baltic peoples.

---

[2] See *Armenian Update* (Zoryan Institute, Cambridge, Mass.), the October 89 and April 90 issues.

[. . .] Conflicts between the three peoples of the Caucasus do not allow for the consolidation of a united posture, as is the case with the Baltic republics. In this respect, it seems that Moscow contributes to the continuation of tensions between the peoples of the Caucasus. On the other hand, when these tensions take on the characteristics of armed conflict and war, they may cost Gorbachev his leadership. Gorbachev is, therefore, interested in maintaining a certain level of tension between the Armenians and Azerbaijanis so that the two or three peoples will not develop a regional and cooperative stand like that of the Baltic states.

Our purpose at the Riga meetings was to become acquainted and engage in a dialogue, and in this regard we reached our goals. To what degree the APF represented the Azerbaijani people is hard to say [. . .] But APF delegates were disturbed by the situation and had the same anxieties as we did, leading to attempts to resolve the situation through negotiations.

We should not measure everybody, not even the Azerbaijanis, by the same yardstick [. . .] I learned that the Azerbaijani Popular Front, as a political organization, does not exist. The APF includes all political forces, from the intellectual fighting against totalitarianism and administrative arbitrariness to the mobs actually involved in the ransacking of Armenian homes. And, depending on the existing political situation, this or that element assumes a leadership role. The APF confessed that they exert a somewhat tangible influence on their people when the political situation is calm. When the situation is exacerbated, the mob takes over. And, by their own account, their organization, unlike the ANM, is unable to assume responsibility for the whole of Azerbaijan.

[. . .] We asked the APF delegates about Pan-Turanism and about the degree to which they wanted to be united with Turkey. "We are a separate people," they said, smiling. "If we are able to secede from the Soviet Union, why would we want to be united with Turkey, or worse, Iran?" Our critics say, "The APF has deceived you." That is their assessment, not ours.

[. . .] On the second day of the meetings we received a telegram from Yerevan saying that APF representatives in Khanlar, accompanied by regional and military representatives, had entered the villages of Azat and Kamo, demanding that villagers leave.[3] We informed [all concerned] that the ANM exec-

---

[3] Armenian villages that are part of Mountainous Karabagh in every respect but are not included within the boundaries of the Autonomous Region of Mountainous Karabagh.

utive committee had decided to suspend the meetings [. . .] We said that it was not possible to continue the meetings [. . .] It was unacceptable that the meetings would be exploited to carry out acts of harassment [. . .] In fact, the army was implementing Gorbachev's solution to the question of Karabagh: To solve the Karabagh issue by depopulating it of its Armenian inhabitants. At first the target was the villages of Azat and Kamo. Had these villages been depopulated, Getashen would be completely surrounded. After Getashen there would be Shaumian, which could not resist long. After Shaumian it would be Karabagh's turn.[4]

[4] Getashen and Shaumian too are just outside the boundaries of the Autonomous Region of Mountainous Karabagh. Strategically they are critical for the defense of the Mountainous Karabagh region itself.

Document Four

VAZGEN MANUKIAN

It Is Time to Jump off the Train

With this article, Vazgen Manukian reconciles the lessons of history on Armenia's liberation with the political exigencies of the present. He argues that independence for Armenia is not only a lofty ideal and a feasible undertaking; it may also be inevitable. Above all, independence is necessary for the nation to define its own national interests and the proper strategy to attain those goals without the manipulation of external powers.

The analysis presented here on the processes in the USSR are equally significant, considering the conventional wisdom in the West which continues to support the central authorities against the republics at any cost.

The text displays what the leadership of the ANM considers its most important asset: The ability to develop a program and strategy based on a realistic assessment of objective realities and of one's own resources.

The article appeared as a series in Hayk *(Nos. 15, 16, 17 and 18, [May-June] 1990), when developments in Moscow were confirming the movement's suspicions regarding the direction of perestroika, while the thought of independence was evoking the worst fears among Armenians concerning a future without a protector and the Armenian National Movement had started to look ahead at the inevitable parliamentary elections.*

No nation, no state can develop economic and political plans based on its own wishes, on its internal reality alone. It is necessary to consider not only the situation of neighbors and the rest of the world but also the likely course of development of world events. We must develop a national agenda and, accordingly, determine the order of problems to be resolved. To predict precisely the course of coming events is, of course, impossible; it is necessary [instead], to examine possible scenarios and intervene at the right moment, occasionally taking intelligent risks without which no problem can be resolved.

If there are no calculations and projections, then [a nation] chooses between two possible courses. It curls up and gives itself to the current, waiting to see what happens (usually nothing good happens on its own); or it has a reflexive reaction—unable to take the uncertain tension—and, with an hysterical enthusiasm, rushes to the slogan "liberty or death."[1] Even if appropriate for the individual, such a reaction is altogether unacceptable for the nation. Both of these courses can be detected in our reality.

Our nation is currently at a critical juncture in its history. We are all evolving toward the conviction that the evolution of events may now make possible the realization of the age-old dream of our people, the reestablishment of political independence, without which practically all other questions of national importance will remain unresolved.

Many are afraid of the opportunities becoming available to us to act in a sovereign manner. The heaviest burden in the world is the burden of making decisions on one's own responsibility. Slavery is sweet in the sense that it relieves one from that burden, and it frees one from the sense of responsibility. A person used to slavery can be intimidated by freedom, by responsibility. It is not incidental that just as we see opening ahead of us opportunities to make decisions regarding the future of our people and to benefit from them, there are people who see hopelessness and speak of a dead end.

No, there is no dead end. There is a difficult road ahead, which has been travelled by many other nations and which leads to happiness. What is needed is cooperation, unity, intelligent calculations, and decisiveness.

Let us now predict the likely path on which the USSR will be moving, the causes of that process, and accordingly, let us see what is possible for us to do and how to do it. What follows is the most widely held position [articulated at this moment] with regard to these questions, a position supported by the Karabagh Committee and subsequently adopted by many other organizations and individuals.

---

1 It is not clear if the author has in mind political forces in Armenia only. But within a few lines Manukian seems to be defining the main characteristics of the two extremes of the Armenian political spectrum within Armenia as well as in the diaspora.

The Soviet Union, at the brink of a deep economic and political crisis, was compelled to implement reforms, to attempt the creation of a democratic society and a free economy. Benefitting from these circumstances, we must strive to achieve economic independence and sovereignty and be ready to declare independence at the appropriate moment.

Nonetheless, independence is frightening many among us because Turkey is a neighbor. (It is interesting that the same people, with intriguing bravura, are constantly speaking of recapturing territories from Turkey.)[2] Because of that [fear], we also see the following position: To strive for a federative status and be satisfied with it. Isn't it true, they argue, that European countries are conceding significant portions of their independence, creating a new form of association? Consequently, [the argument continues] that is what we should be emulating.

We must note that in order to concede something you must first have that thing; it is only when you have it that you are able to determine what and to whom you concede, in whose name and in return for what you make your concessions. Secondly, the substance and legal definition of independence change from century to century. There are processes taking place now in Europe in which just about all countries of the world are participating, wherein first there are clusters of states which are later dissolved into a worldwide unit. The meaning of independence in the twenty-first century will be determined through these processes.

Let us also note that the federative style of state formation is an unstable one; and almost all of the federations known to history (the Swiss federation, the USA, the German confederation, etc.) have evolved along the same path: Confederation at first, then federation, and finally evolution into a unitary, single statehood.

Let us now focus on the processes taking place in the USSR and see whether the above position, according to which it is possible to achieve independence by first evolving toward sovereignty, is valid.

To understand what is taking place within the USSR, the likely course of its development, and the causes for the current movement, let us briefly review history.

Throughout centuries of Russian history, there have been many changes in regimes but one aspect has remained consistent:

---

[2] The reference is mainly to diaspora organizations but also to more recent statements by Armenia's Communist Party.

Its expansionist politics. In the course of its expansion, Russia reached us and took some of our territories.[3] We must be aware that Russia's coming to Armenia had nothing to do with our appeals or our orientation.[4] Russia was accomplishing its own "mission," [implementing its own policy of] expansionism. (It is interesting to note that some of the peoples conquered along the path of this expansionism had living standards higher than those enjoyed by Russians. This phenomenon which has deep causes, which must be set aside as [it can be] the subject of another discussion.)

The internal logic of the politics of conquest led Russia to a politics of intolerance toward the creation of independent statehoods; Russia did everything possible to ensure that the conquered nations had no opportunity to create independent statehoods. For that purpose Russia pursued a policy of Russification in the conquered territories: Russification of language and culture; mixed marriages, etc. Where this policy did not succeed, everything was done to make sure that the given people did not constitute a majority in its own lands. Deportations, massacres, and repopulation of conquered lands by Russians were all aimed at [producing] a demographic change [favorable to Russia].

For that reason, objectively, the realization of our age old dream of a united and independent Armenia was in conflict with the interests of Russia. That is also one of the most important reasons why we were unsuccessful in securing the physical survival of a significant portion of our brothers at the end of the last and the beginning of this century.[5] (The role and interests of Turkey in this matter are a matter of record; we are now discussing Russia.) [We were unable to secure physical survival], when physical survival had been achieved for centuries under very difficult circumstances within the Ottoman Turkish and Safawid Persian empires.[6]

Let us now note that if expansionist Russia was a natural enemy of our national ideals, a Russia that abstains from such a policy provides us with opportunities to create that statehood. A new, democratic Russia can become a natural ally of our statehood. Expansionist Russia is, objectively, our enemy.

---

3 Eastern Armenia, a small portion of historic Armenia formerly under Safawid Persian rule, was annexed by Russia in 1827- 1828.

4 See Document One, notes 7 and 10.

5 Reference to the Genocide of Armenians in the Ottoman Empire during the First World War.

6 The implication is that Russia had a major share of responsibility in the Genocide.

Some think that if, in its expansionist phase, Russia had reached all the way to Van[7] and then had collapsed, perhaps we could have won more. But, to begin with, if Russia had conquered those lands, we would still be where we are now; there would have been no Armenians left on those territories (it is likely that Turkish and Kurdish republics would have been erected on those lands); the history of the First World War, or of Nakhichevan[8] are proof of this. Secondly, there is no expectation that such a scenario will evolve in the foreseeable future. Expansionist politics is now in contradiction to the direction of world affairs, and the USSR has no means to develop such a policy. Moreover, denied statehood, we may wait indecisively for a change in the direction of world affairs in favor of expansionism—if such a phase can still return—so that Russia can become actively expansionist again while we continue to link such nonsensical hopes to this expansionism; [but we will have to wait so long that] by that time we will have ceased to exist as a nation.

A democratic Russia can be our ally. Yet it is possible to have allies only when you have an independent state. History and politics encompass laws that are not dependent on the wishes of individuals. One of these is a law that is simple yet important for our discussion: World affairs during every historical period follow a course of development characteristic for that period; and if the direction of the foreign and domestic policies of a state fails to coincide with that general course of development, within that state will evolve forces that will destroy that state. The more these policies deviate from the general direction, the more powerful the destructiveness of these forces. These emerging forces, consciously or otherwise, act as corrective mechanisms that bring the wayward state to the general fold. Only by applying great resources, by using much energy, can the leaders of that state resist—even then, only temporarily—the corrective forces, and [this is done at the cost of] condemning the country to economic, political, military, scientific, cultural and moral stagnation. The longer the stagnation lasts, the more powerful will be the explosion. Events in Rumania can serve as an example.[9]

---

[7] City in southwest Turkey, capital of a medieval kingdom and center of modern nationalism. In 1915 Armenians there distinguished themselves by a spirited defense of the city against the threat of deportations and massacres. The defenders were finally saved by the Armenian volunteers in the Russian army.

[8] See Document One, note 75.

[9] Reference to former President Ceaucescu's refusal in 1989 to relinquish power

As a consequence of the First World War, certain empires collapsed and were transformed into new states whose course of development more or less followed the direction dominant in the world. Turkey and Austria-Hungary are examples. Great Britain, Spain, Portugal, and others adopted the same course following the Second World War. And now we are witnessing the [collapse of the] last of these dinosaurs, Russia.

Currently the dominant course in the development of world affairs is the strengthening of [nation] states [through] scientific, technical, economic, and cultural development. One magic word describes the foundation of that course: Freedom. And all attempts to go against that direction, regardless of what lofty and powerful ideals may be used as arguments to justify such attempts, are condemned to fail. One can cite the communist and fascist ideologies as examples of such failures.

Now it is Russia's turn. As stated above, for centuries Russia has pursued an expansionist policy, ceaselessly, while changing forms of government; the last of these changes was bolshevism. The last attempt at expansion, Afghanistan, was a failure.[10] The last form of government engendered a crisis in all areas of life. Moreover, countries such as Poland and Hungary, loosely tied to the empire, began to sever their ties gradually. The empire had already lost the power to keep them in. The world was watching with horror this disintegrating giant which had the weight to smother the rest of mankind under its rubble. The world was arming, preparing to defend itself against a likely holocaust as it watched the empire on its death bed.

There was one way to avoid the explosion: To introduce quick changes in the domestic and foreign policies of the country while keeping the course of change under control. There arose the problem: How to change the system of government, adjust the country's direction to that of the rest of the world, and secure the development of science and technology and of military and economic production in the context of new conditions, without sustaining major territorial losses or having to introduce radical changes within the government? There appeared in Russia an individual who took upon himself the task of answer-

when faced with a popular uprising and his attempt to repress it by force.

10 Former USSR President Leonid Brezhnev ordered the Soviet army into Afghanistan in December 1979. The invasion was opposed by the successful guerrilla war of the *mujahideen* supported by the West. Gorbachev changed Soviet policy. Withdrawal of Soviet forces began in May 1988 and was completed in less than a year.

ing that question. That individual was Mikhail Gorbachev.[11]

If, at the beginning, it appeared that reform was possible through minor and formal changes, in time it became clear that the changes and losses would be great. Even worse, it also became clear that the course and pace of changes could not be kept under full control. We should not deceive ourselves. It is Gorbachev himself who is destroying the old way of government, the government under the leadership of the Communist Party, by pushing the people forward. That question is not altogether resolved; but it is obvious that the communist method of government is condemned. For natural reasons the disappearance of that system is taking place at different speeds in different regions of the country. Since he would like to preserve the territorial integrity of the empire as much as possible, it is in Gorbachev's interest that the process move more slowly in the outlying areas of the Union. Moreover, there is a very clever attempt to supplant the national liberation struggles of conquered peoples—which, as a natural course, should have been directed against [Russia's] imperialism—with struggles against the system of government of the empire. In other words, the central authorities are attempting to replace national liberation struggles that would be aiming at independence with anticommunist struggles.

Benefitting from their distinct and particular conditions, it became possible for some republics, such as Lithuania, to carry on the correct struggle. Lithuanians distinguished imperialist policy [Russian expansionism] from the method of its execution [Communism] and found a masterful balance between the two goals. I am not speaking in defense of the Communist Party. The Communist Party is an organization guilty of crimes committed against humanity and against our people, and it must disappear from the political arena. I am merely appealing to our senses so that we may coldly calculate the direction of our political struggle.

Having been forced to destroy the old system of government, having sustained territorial losses in Eastern Europe and the Baltics,[12] Gorbachev is attempting to erect a unified democratic state on the remaining territories, a state whose economy is led by the principle of free market. He wants to create a unified and stable country which can avoid disintegration and whose

---

[11] Mikhail S. Gorbachev (b. 1931) was elected First Secretary of the Communist Party of the Soviet Union in March 1985 and initiated the policies of perestroika and glasnost.

[12] Lithuania, Latvia, Estonia.

course of development is as close as possible to that of the rest of the world.

Will Gorbachev be able to solve that problem? And what awaits us along the path of discovery of the answer to that question?

As mentioned above, the incompatibility of the direction of USSR politics with that of the rest of the world produced forces within the country that began to destroy the empire. The economy was becoming unmanageable; it was becoming impossible to implement decisions taken at the center. Official ideology, which had played an important role in the government of the country, was slowly losing its effectiveness. Economic decline and the fall of oil prices on the international market were making it difficult to hold tightly to the socialist countries through a variety of injections. A national liberation struggle started in Poland. Then there were the failures in Afghanistan. And the USSR was falling increasingly behind most countries of the world in the areas of economic, scientific, and new technological development. These declines could not but affect the most important characteristic of the USSR, its military production and its military might. There was danger in the realization that time was running against the USSR and that could lead the leadership to adventurous behavior; the Soviet leadership could use its military capabilities to ensure that the rest of the world does not pass it by. But the gerontocracy governing the country did not have that resolve; perhaps more, it had the circumspection to avoid that route, which could have been destructive for all of mankind. In this respect the policy and resolve of the United States and of its then president Ronald Reagan not to be blackmailed and [American] application to military purposes of the most advanced technological tools played a major role.[13]

The leadership of the USSR thus followed a policy of "extending its feet the length of its cover" and tried to reach the rest of the world by a policy of reforms. At the beginning, that policy had an element of pretense, a wish to achieve major goals through minor adjustments. But events forced all to see that changes must be radical, while losses of territories conquered by previous regimes could be substantial. This realization opened the way for a series of events whose direction and pace cannot be controlled by the center; and the use of army and KGB personnel for that purpose is not producing the necessary results.

When the government started giving up on the idea of man-

---

[13] Refers to the Strategic Defense Initiative or "Star Wars."

aging the economy through the administrative-bureaucratic control system, the pace of economic disintegration quickened; it may yet bring about economic and political chaos. On the other hand, the reforms intended to bring about the free market system and private ownership are being postponed constantly. And we know that once these reforms are implemented, the first phase will bring about huge inflation and unemployment, developments which in this multinational empire will have unpredictable political consequences. It is also obvious that when such reforms are implemented in the economic arena, the whole of the economy will be out of the control of the country's leadership and this will mean that the leadership is also incapable of exerting authority in the political arena.

Under the circumstances we, but also the leadership of the country which has at its disposal far more powerful means of affecting the course of events, will be unable to calculate or predict how events will develop and what will be the impact of this or that policy decision. It is only possible to mention a few possible scenarios.

Before we move on to a discussion of these likely scenarios, let us speak about wishes. It is possible to deduce from Gorbachev's policies that he wishes to erect a unified state covering the whole of the present USSR, which, being compatible with the general direction of the rest of the world, may be similar to the structure of the USA; that he wishes the country to be divided into such parts (republics, autonomous regions, regions tied to Russia) which individually would enjoy roughly the same freedoms and rights as are enjoyed by each state of the USA.

Judging from the statements and policies of Western leaders, the West is interested in seeing Gorbachev's goal achieved. The reasons for that position are clear. The West desires a neighbor whose democratic structure and open economic system do not threaten the West's military security, instead of an aggressive, large empire that has military power but a closed and stagnant economy or instead of a group of small, economically weak, nationalistic and warring states—once that empire disintegrates. The West's visualization also assumes the the Soviet Union will constitute a gigantic market. Therefore, for pragmatic reasons, the West at the present time, unlike in the preceding period, is not encouraging the separatist politics of certain constituent republics of the USSR.[14] Nonetheless, consider-

---

[14] Republics have become the driving force of most reforms currently being attempted in the Soviet Union, while the central government has focused

ing world public opinion, Western leaders do occasionally make statements or even take action based on such universal values as liberty, the right of self-determination of nations, etc. Furthermore, the West is concerned that the centrifugal movement of republics may lead the USSR toward chaos with unpredictable and dangerous consequences not only for the empire but also for the West. Finally, the West is apprehensive of a Soviet return to its former policies.

Thus, on these questions, the wishes of the West and those of Gorbachev coincide. But it is all the same, since these wishes cannot be fully realized. The empire cannot avoid sustaining territorial losses. The inevitability of the secession of the Baltic republics is one example. All of Russia is already coming to terms with that idea.

Three factors make it impossible to create a USA-like state on the territory of the USSR.

a) Unlike the USA, many constituent elements of the USSR are nations that have been made part of the USSR along with their historic homelands; the desire of such peoples to create their own future again is too strong.

b) The economic reforms that must be introduced and which must, at least initially, be accompanied by a lower standard of living, will strengthen centrifugal forces. Each republic, naturally based on its own interests, will try to develop its economy at the expense of the others. The rich will not want to share with the poor.

c) It is also natural to think that it will be easier to introduce economic reforms in different parts of the country in different forms and at different paces rather than uniformly throughout the huge expanse of the empire.

Let us now see what is it that we want.

It is obvious that Russia will not disappear from the face of the earth and that, sooner or later, a unified Russia will be rebuilt on the largest remnant of the collapsing empire. Let us set aside the questions such as the number of phases the process will require, the number of victims the process will take, and what tragedies will be incurred along the path. Let us assume an almost fantastic scenario that we succeeded in going through all the disasters along the way and became part of the unified democratic Russia that was rebuilt.

largely on an attempt to stop the disintegration of the empire. But Western governments, as well as segments of the media and academia, continue to present the republican efforts as "nationalistic" as a means to bolster Gorbachev's position from abroad.

Is this something we want? In my opinion, no. If that unlikely scenario comes to pass and we are part of a democratic Russia, that will mark the end of the millennia-old history of the Armenian people, just as we have seen the end of the national history of Wales and Scotland. These two countries still harbor, of course, political parties that aim for independence, but their widespread Anglification, the principle of equality under the law, and high standard of living dominant in Great Britain have led the Scots and the Welsh to the point where the majority of both peoples consider independence merely an exotic idea. Thus, these peoples have been pushed out of the arena of world history and, just as today there no Sumerians, Arameans, etc.,[15] similarly, after a while, there will not be any Scots or Welsh. Do we want to accept the same fate? We Armenians have seen how the pyramids of Egypt were built, we have fought the Assyrians and ancient Romans; during Tigran the Great we reached the Red Sea,[16] we witnessed and participated in the birth and development of universal religions such as Christianity and Islam, we have seen the rise and fall of the strongest empires; we have given much to the world and have endured a lot while passing through a road full of trials and tribulations. But it is my deeply felt belief that all is still ahead of us and that we have still not fulfilled the mission for which God placed us on this earth, and it would constitute a sacrilege to God, to mankind, and to our forefathers if we fail to carry our cross by realizing the goal of independence at the first opportunity presented to us.

Therefore, the first scenario we looked at—the fantastic possibility that surviving the holocausts awaiting the development of a democratic and unified Russia by some miracle, to be part of it—is not something that we wish to see. We must strive to reconstitute our independent statehood.

From wishes and fantastic hypotheses, let us return to our current realities.

The USSR, forced by serious considerations, is moving from one stable era to another. We are now in the transitional phase.

---

[15] Various peoples of the ancient world.

[16] Most famous of Armenian kings (Artashesian Dynasty, 95 - 55B.C. Tigran, or Tigranes, benefitted from a temporary lull in Roman-Persian rivalry and warfare to extend his rule toward the Mediterranean. This "empire" lasted about six years and ended in 69 B.C.

For Armenians, denied statehood and lacking military resources in a world defined by nation-states and empires, achievements in history, however distant, have acquired a particular significance. In this respect no other figure in Armenian history matches the value of "Tigran the Great."

It is important to realize that secession is possible only during the transitional phase. Secession is not a characteristic development during a stable situation. Therefore, we must realize our desire for the reestablishment of statehood during this transitional period, whose duration is still unknown.

Now let us look at the possible scenarios.

1. The British Model

This model is the most desirable yet the least likely scenario: Events in the USSR follow the same course as in Great Britain at the end of the Second World War, i.e. all conquered nations gradually acquire their independence almost without a struggle. Such a course is the most desirable for us, since it gives us the opportunity not to hasten events, to develop our economy step by step, to create a healthy moral environment within the republic, to free ourselves from the mores forced upon us for seventy years, to return to our national roots, to consolidate the nuclei of democracy, one way or the other to resolve the question of Karabagh and, after that, at the appropriate moment, leave the USSR. I find such a development highly unlikely for the following reasons:

a) The economic instability already mentioned above seems to leave little room for an orderly resolution.

b) In creating an empire, England was motivated by a set of pragmatic goals characteristic to Anglo-Saxons, the pursuit of material gain; when the changes in the world order and technological revolution opened new prospects for development whereby economic development was no longer conditioned by [ownership] of colonies, England released its colonies without a struggle.

The case is somewhat different for Russia. In this country, the policy of conquest had another peculiar motivation. Of course, Russia benefitted economically from the natural resources of countries it conquered; but that was not the reason which pushed Russia ahead. There is a deeply held belief among the Russian people that by conducting a policy of conquest and by expanding, they were executing a mission imposed upon them by God and that they are bringing happiness to peoples they conquer and Russify. It will not be easy for Russia to forfeit such a quasi-mystical national philosophy.

c) Even England did not give up those conquered territories that constituted an extension of its own national patrimony. It relinquished southern Ireland with much difficulty; Northern Ireland is still struggling. Scotland and Wales were never liberated. And [in the case of the USSR] the territories currently in question are all contiguous to Russia itself and it is obvious that Russia will not relinquish them easily.

In discussing the English model, I find it necessary to note a general rule that applies even to those colonies that acquired their independence with little difficulty. Colonies first declared their intention to attain independence and then began negotiations with the British. During negotiations they would agree on the period of transition at which time alone there would be a step-by-step move toward sovereignty. Consequently, experience shows that even if events develop according to this unlikely scenario, it will be necessary at some point to show resolve and officially declare our intention to obtain independence. Following such a declaration, and in the event of an agreement with the center, it becomes possible to develop an independent economy.

2. The "Stop and Go" Model

Let us look at this more likely model of change. It is very probable that the path toward the creation of a unified democratic Russia will consist of a number of phases. If the USSR is able to make even slight progress in overcoming its current problems, to make minor adjustments in adjusting its course to that of the rest of the world, to raise even by a small measure the standard of living of its people, and to come close to integrating some of the modern technologies, there will be forces (most probably led by Gorbachev himself) that will have an interest in not continuing the course of reforms and being satisfied with what has been achieved. The doors will then once again close against those peoples who had not seceded from the empire; and what will remain is a semi-democratic state that will remain as such until the next adjustment toward the direction of the rest of the world.

And thus, [we would continue] phase by phase, each phase laden with its own unpredictable disasters, while national assimilation continues during the intervening periods. [There would be] explosion after explosion, each explosion potentially [capable of] bringing our national existence to an end. Under these circumstances, the reestablishment of national statehood is not only a means to pursue noble goals or liberation from slavery and provide opportunities for a better life; it also becomes the only means to secure the physical existence of our people.

3. The "Destruction" Model

When describing the current situation of the USSR, I have already stated that the economy of the country is at an impasse. Centrifugal forces have become more powerful, too many issues have become unmanageable—all of which may bring about the collapse of the empire.

Any attempt to bring about an end to this course of events by crude military intervention may produce a temporary halt but it will also produce, inevitably, chaos and explosion as well as a faster pace of collapse. In this case, the danger for us is that we may remain under the rubble of the collapsed empire. It is desirable that our independence not come as a result of that explosion; rather, that we face that collapse as an independent state, recognized by the other states of the world.

In addition to the obvious advantages, there is yet another that must be mentioned. Our neighbor Turkey is exerting efforts to follow the general direction of development by replacing external conquest with a policy of internal development and to become a modern, developed country (and we must confess that it has made serious progress in that respect). But we cannot rule out the possibility that, in the case of a collapse of an ungovernable USSR, elements that currently have little political weight in Turkey[17] may raise their heads and the country may temporarily deviate from its above-mentioned course, absorb those parts of the collapsing USSR that are accessible to it, and then return to its path [of internal development].

In the case of such a collapse there may also be a danger from other neighbors within the USSR that may attempt to absorb sections of the empire. Understandably, we would have major advantages if we are independent by then, such as in the area of defense and in the solution of other questions of national importance.

This is a likely scenario if, despite the efforts of the USSR leadership and the desires of the West, it becomes impossible to change the current course toward unmanageability and prevent the collapse by chaos and implosion. In this matter, the self-control of forces at play within the USSR—the abstention from egotistic tendencies for the benefit of the general good—is very important. To illustrate this point, let us take the example of the Baltic republics. By benefitting from the opportune moment and, in my opinion, making the right calculations, the Baltic

---

[17] The reference is to Pan-Turkists. See Document One, note 6. During the last parliamentary elections in Turkey, the Pan-Turkists won 1% of the popular vote.

states took a decisive step and, each in its own way, declared independence.[18] And although they are still not independent and the process may take some years, the important task is accomplished: They have set themselves apart in case of a collapse of the Soviet empire. They have realized the wish of their people, and they have established the possibility of autonomous development. By doing so, the Baltic republics placed the other peoples of the USSR in a difficult position, increased the level of tension in the country, and removed an important link in the chain of peoples in need of liberation—peoples who are trying to achieve independence from the empire shoulder-to-shoulder, step-by-step. Is it possible to accuse the Baltic peoples of egotism? Maybe yes, maybe not; that is not the essential point. The simplest rule in politics is that when you have an opportunity to realize a national ideal, you are obligated to benefit from that moment immediately, and not to sacrifice the national interest in the name of others. Later it may be too late. History does not forgive those who do not benefit from available opportunities. These are the cruel laws of history and we must submit to them, whether we like them or not.

The examination of this model indicates that the likelihood of its becoming reality is very high.

[The previous analyses indicate] that we must secede as soon as possible, because slowing down may be dangerous for the survival of our people. It is necessary to speed up [the process of attaining independence] also for yet another reason.

The mentality that we can develop our economy by staying within the structure of the USSR and then secede is baseless. This approach is one of the baits used to keep us in the empire until they settle their affairs, i.e. a bait for the transitional period. The truth is they are giving us a certain amount of supplies and raw materials against which they will be demanding higher and higher prices while, on the other hand, they are making it impossible for us to develop our own economy by passing more and more laws. We can overcome some of these obstacles, of course, by waging a major struggle. But then there will be new laws and our Supreme Soviet will be preoccupied by sending protest notes, by constant confrontations with Moscow, always with minimal results. The most important factor in the decision of the Baltic states to speed up their declaration of independence was their realization that it was impossible to

---

[18] Lithuania began the process by declaring unilateral independence in March 1990. Each in its own way, Latvia and Estonia followed.

develop their economy while staying within the Union. The economy of the USSR will continue to roll down this economic abyss for a long time to come, pulling us down with it, and offering no prospect of development.

When on our own, we may at first fall faster into the abyss; but not being tied to the disintegrated economy of that large country, we can also pull out much faster. Here, our sovereignty, our spirit of initiative, and our diaspora will play important roles.

Therefore we must speed up the process of our independence. At this point, we must deal with the question of the feasibility of realizing that independence. It is true that staying within the USSR is providing us with no prospects for the future, and slowing down may be dangerous for us. But it is equally true that it is dangerous to hastily take steps that are not well thought-out. We have the bitter historical experience of taking hasty steps in a collapsing empire.[19]

We noted above that it will be difficult for the Russian people (as is to some extent true for all expansionist peoples) to give up any portion of conquered territory. Just as [is the case with] its psychology of conquest, an important role is also played here by the desire of the Russian people to continue benefitting politically and militarily from the occupied lands. But at the present moment there is a curious psychological mood among Russians which is useful for our purposes. Russia's immersion in its own problems has momentarily eclipsed its imperial tendencies and instincts. The search for culprits to hold responsible for the economic disaster, and the Russians' need to come out of that disaster, have led them to the conclusion that, so far, it is they who were serving the conquered peoples. It is now the Russians who wish to abdicate from the role of bringing "happiness" to the conquered peoples; they wish to pursue their economic interests, somewhat hurt by the actions of "ungrateful" [formerly colonial] peoples to whom they are saying, "Go and keep your own heads above water." Also, the events and revelations of the last two years about Russian policies of [state terror] have produced a sense of guilt among some Russians and now they also seem to be trying to prove that they are abandoning such policies, that they are willing to give freedom to these peoples [. . .][20]

Gorbachev was correct when in one of his speeches he said

---

[19] Refers to the Genocide in the Ottoman Empire.

[20] Boris Yeltsin (See note 22) is reported to have made statements in this respect on many occasions.

that imperialism is genetically ingrained in Russians. I even suspect that among all these objective factors Gorbachev, too, may have something to do with the change in the mood.

The issue is that, as pointed out earlier, Gorbachev is trying to resolve two mutually exclusive problems simultaneously. On the one hand, he wants to secure the democratic, economic development of the country, following the dominant course of development around the world. On the other hand, through unequal development, treachery, the use of military force, and baits aimed at economic benefits and advantages in the nationalities question, he is trying to keep the territorial integrity of the empire. Now being convinced that the two cannot be resolved at the same time and, in my opinion, giving priority to the question of general development, Gorbachev is resigned to some loss of territory. The less, the better, of course. But that is possible only if the Russian people itself agrees to it. On the one hand, the idea of loss of territory is gradually introduced among the Russians, while Gorbachev himself unexpectedly talks about not giving up land "conquered by the blood of forefathers."[21] That is the politics favored by Gorbachev. He first introduces the issue, creates public opinion, then he starts to control [the debate] so that the matter does not evolve dangerously and acquire major proportions, discusses the contrary course, and secures for himself an alibi. It is possible to mention many examples. To mention just one: His treatment of the issue of the multiparty system. When in 1988 he unexpectedly started saying that there was no need for parties other than the Communist Party, it became clear to many that the end of the monopoly of power of the Communists was near. Gorbachev constantly ascribes to himself the role of the restrainer, a role that is adjusted to the particular political situation at hand. It is not even important whether he is conscious of his tactics or if it happens at the instinctive level. Looking at it from the sidelines, one can only admire the cleverness with which it is done. Therefore, along with real reasons for the change among Russians in their disposition toward imperialism, one must also take into consideration the role of the game Gorbachev plays. It was Yeltsin[22] who benefitted most adroitly from the current

---

[21] With the resignation of Foreign Minister Eduard Shevardnadze at the end of 1990, it was less certain that Gorbachev was willing to accept any territorial losses or that he placed reforms above all other considerations.

[22] Boris Yeltsin is a former associate of Gorbachev in the ruling Politburo. He lost his power when he criticized Gorbachev for being too timid in his reforms. Yeltsin returned to the political scene as President of the Russian Federation

mood in Russia; he acquired great political weight by the increase in the level of instability within the USSR.

This is not to say that Gorbachev will agree to the independence of Armenia without any kind of resistance or that the Russian people will resign to it easily.

In my opinion, we have simply entered an era propitious for the raising of the question of our independence, an era that may not last long. The way we raise that question does have a decisive significance though.

It will be unacceptable for the USSR and dangerous for us if we follow the example of Lithuania. Here the following factors play a role:

1. The USSR has different strategic concerns in Europe, the Caucasus, and Central Asia. Because the USSR's decision to adjust to the course followed by the rest of the world aims at entering the European market, territories lost in Europe will continue somehow to be tied to the USSR (although much more loosely than before). In the case of the Caucasus, some of the liberated peoples of that region may end up in economic groupings with other countries (and here Turkey's relations to the world/European Community will be an important issue).[23] It is much more dangerous to lose the Central Asian territories because the latter will certainly end up as parts of other economic and political groupings and will be lost to Russia for good.

2. The Caucasus region is a much older conquest for Russia than the Baltic republics.[24] Not only Russia, but the West, too, are inclined to see those regions [the Caucasus] as inseparable parts of Russia. Moreover, some countries have as yet not recognized the Soviet annexation of the Baltic republics. One should also remember that, given the nonviolent strategy adopted by the Baltic peoples, any military intervention there on the part of Russia will bring back vivid memories of the USSR's interventions in Europe (Hungary, Czechoslovakia) and will be actively resisted by the West. This is not something Gorbachev can ignore. He may lose the important moral capital accumu-

and has since assumed a major role in Soviet affairs.

[23] Turkey has made membership in the European Market a major foreign policy objective. Turkey's application was denied in 1990, but may be reconsidered at a later date, depending on the role it plays in the resolution of the Gulf crisis since Iraq's occupation of Kuwait and on the way that conflict is resolved. See Document One, note 74.

[24] The Baltic republics were annexed during the Second World War. Russian annexation of the Transcaucasus began in 1801 with Georgia and was completed in 1828.

lated during the previous years. Military intervention in the Caucasus has become common and is accepted in the West with "understanding."[25] Military intervention here is disturbing to some degree only to the immediate neighbors—Iran and Turkey. At any time, it is possible to create ethnic disturbances in the Caucasus, and the use of military force will be seen as "justified" and be treated with silence in the West.

Currently there is only one path for us toward independence, and that is the constitutional path. This course gives us an opportunity to work out differences with the center at the level of more or less confrontational politics and does not allow the center to resort, at least openly, to inimical means against us.[26] It is true that everything was done in order to create doubts among our people with regard to the constitutional means, but we have no other recourse.

The USSR Supreme Soviet has adopted a very complex law regarding the right of secession of soviet republics. It appears that taking advantage of that law is the only choice we have to secede from the USSR.[27] We must resort to that law. We should not at the present time get into the details of the application of that law. Let us simply note that before we begin to use that law, we must go through a preparatory period of explanation with the people, and then, there must be an unofficial referendum to determine the opinions of the people regarding secession. Only after that can the Supreme Soviet of Armenia resort to that law and take decisive action. But we

[25] American and Western officials have stated consistently that the use of force by the central authorities in republics was acceptable if the purpose was to stop ethnic strife. US Secretary of State James Baker stated on November 29, 1989, for example, that while the US opposes the use of force to reverse reforms in Eastern Europe, it could support Kremlin moves, including imposition of martial law, to end unrest in the republics of Armenia and Azerbaijan. The most recent statement in this vein was made through the US Department of State on January 9, 1991.

[26] After Lithuania declared its independence, President Gorbachev proposed, and the USSR Congress of People's Deputies approved, a constitutional amendment requiring elaborate steps before a republic could secede. The steps required included a waiting period, a popular referendum, detailed negotiations, and a vote by the People's Congress. In pursuing its course toward independence, Armenia has functioned largely within the provisions of this amendment. However, as in other instances, the amendment has become largely irrelevant as it is overtaken by events. Gorbachev appears now to give priority to the goal of keeping the empire intact at any cost; he makes laws and principles irrelevant by using them for tactical purposes and then discarding them.

[27] Refers to new secession law. See next note.

must hurry. The opportunity given us may not be repeated. History does not forgive those who are late. After taking the initial steps we have the right to negotiate with the USSR authorities to establish the new, semi-independent status, which, according to the law, can last five years. That status gives far wider opportunities to take steps should the situation change drastically. Let us set aside, for a moment, the question as to what sort of counterattack the USSR can initiate in case we demand the application of the law of secession. Let us, rather, see what is it that we want from the USSR when we sit to negotiate, what can the interim status give us, when we are still part of the USSR but are to some degree on our own.[28]

Meanwhile let us note that the act of moving toward independence will facilitate the improvement of our relations with our neighbors. A move toward independence will also invite the attention of the world.[29] World attention isn't something we should be enchanted with; but we should derive from it any benefit we can. Moreover, were we to achieve it, and were Russia able to accept that fact, attaining a semi-independent status will change our position from an ignored slave to that of a partner who has strategic importance in the eyes of Russia itself.[30]

What is the program we must realize during that transitional period? In the economic arena, we must effectuate a sharp turn to private ownership and the free market system. We must adopt the private and public [stock] controlled forms of ownership of land and means of production, an open door policy for foreign capital, and special [laws] guaranteeing the inalienability of private property. It is necessary not only to encourage joint ventures but also the direct investment of foreign companies in our republic in the form of companies established and owned by them. That is the current path of development throughout the

---

[28] Gorbachev has made the constitutional amendment irrelevant by offering a new Union treaty in December 1990. Armenia, among other republics, has stated that it will not sign the new arrangement as too little, too late. See Document Nine, the November 1990 speech by President Levon Ter Petrosian to the USSR Congress of People's Deputies.

[29] Armenia's Declaration on Independence (Document Seven), while not a declaration of independence, attracted much less attention in the West than the author anticipated, as the West had determined not to encourage independence movements or take any step that might appear to weaken Gorbachev's position. Taking note of such declarations was perceived as doing both.

[30] This assumption has been proven largely valid. Armenia's bargaining position has improved in the political arena in the labyrinth of developing new relations between the central authorities and the republics.

whole world. After a while, we too, can have companies in other countries.[31]

It is necessary that the transition to private property and free market systems be done very quickly and decisively, that we be ahead of the USSR.[32] That will help minimize the inflation characteristic of the period of transition from state to private ownership. At first, the inflation caused by the changes we bring about will be spread over the vast volume of Soviet money, producing little change. But then we must accelerate the pace by printing our own money, otherwise the weakened status of the Soviet economy and therefore, of Soviet money, will be an obstacle to the development of our own money. In other words, we must hang on to Soviet money when we are falling in the abyss and rely on our own when we are rising out of the abyss. Life will be difficult for a while, but then it will improve. Some may insist that it is possible to devise an economic program which will bring about an improvement in the material well-being of the people without going through a drop in the standard of living. Such an insistence only indicates that they either do not understand economics or that they are lying and trying to please the public and build political capital. There will be difficulties, but there is no other road (were we to stay within the USSR, the difficulties would be more serious and would last longer).

The state and benevolent societies must assume responsibility in softening the blows on the poor. It is necessary to realize that only economic development makes social justice possible. Dividing up the little that is available creates equal poverty and brings an end to development. We must create the conditions necessary so that people can get rich, and get rich by establishing work places for honest labor and private commercial and industrial concerns, and not by pillaging. It is the responsibility of the state to ensure that the poor are not too poor, that they

---

[31] This is one of the few discussions on economic issues by leaders of the Armenian National Movement. One reason for this paucity is the belief that ultimately the resolution of problems such as economic reform and self-determination for Mountainous Karabagh will be possible when Armenia is a sovereign state with a democratic government. Also, in a futile attempt at relegitimizing itself before it was displaced in August 1990, the Communist led government of Armenia had already stated that it wanted to introduce radical economic reforms, including a market economy. It went as far as advocating free economic zone status for Armenia. There was not much more that the movement could propose, as long as discussion was limited to general principles.

[32] Here too the movement is closer to Yeltsin's position. See also Document Eight.

have the means to have a decent life, and to ensure that the rich do not use their wealth to establish monopoly of power.[33]

Once we have our own money, it is necessary to invite international finance institutions to Armenia to help develop the country. Generally speaking, the greater the number of countries which invest in Armenia, the greater the number of countries with whom we have economic ties, the greater will be the number of countries interested in our independence. Private ownership of land and means of production will create a sector within the population whose interest in independence is based on self-interest, not just on devotion to noble ideals.[34]

The development of economic ties with all of our neighbors, creating opportunities to profit from their transportation networks, and deriving mutual profits are, of course, essential for our economic development. Economic ties with Turkey do not contradict our national interests and, according to some reports, Turkey too considers such ties to be in its own interest.[35] It is possible to cite many examples where even complex political conflicts have not stopped countries from trading with each

---

[33] Capital is most likely to be found among those formerly in positions of power. The trend is for former officials to become the capitalists of the new system as transition to a market economy begins.

[34] This correlation between capital and patriotism may be an oversimplification. For reasons that deserve a separate discussion, the trend in Armenian history has been for capitalists to transfer their capital and skills to safe havens rather than use economic means to create the necessary political and military pre-conditions for the safety of one's capital. This trend has been one of the main reasons for the economic decline of the Armenian plateau over the centuries.

During the last three hundred years there have been occasions for patriotism to evolve from concern for capital. The attempt at the creation of an Armenia by the Armenian merchants in India in the 18th century is one such example. See Document One, notes 11 and 14.

Ultimately, commitment to Armenia and willingness to fight for it, will follow political stability and confidence with regard to the future, not precede it. This places a huge burden on any government, and more so on a government that is democratic.

[35] This suggestion is now policy for Armenia's new government led by Vazgen Manukian. Turkey and Armenia have exchanged trade delegations and Armenia's Vice-Minister for Foreign Affairs met with Turkey's Ambassador to the USSR in Moscow.

The policy is in collision with diasporan attitudes. Political parties there have a formal policy of boycotting Turkish goods. While such statements have symbolic value and their impact on Turkish economy and Armenian thinking is altogether negligible, political parties in the diaspora have criticized openly and severely the Armenian government's policy of developing relations with Turkey before the latter recognizes the Genocide.

other. With regard to the establishment of political and diplomatic ties between Turkey and Armenia, it is clear that, in future negotiations, we will make it a condition that Turkey recognize the Genocide of 1915 with all concomitant consequences. It is obvious that Turkey will present its own conditions. I am aware that this proposal will not be accepted enthusiastically among Armenians, especially among diaspora Armenians. Anti-Turkism has played a certain role among Armenians in the diaspora, for decades, in the task of identity preservation.[36] It is difficult to return to the realpolitik, often the very subtle politics conducted by the leaders of the republic during 1918-1920.[37] But we need that realpolitik, time does not wait. It would be idiocy for us, when we have only four neighbors, to abstain voluntarily from developing economic ties with one of them, and by that to limit our ability to maneuver. To establish trade with Turkey does not mean to forget the Genocide of 1915 nor to forget our historic lands. There is more to be said on this issue.

Experience everywhere indicates that the most important ingredient in the development of an economy and, in general, a country, is the human being. Countries that followed national plans by building huge steel mills remained poor. Those that used borrowed money to prepare specialists are now making great progress toward economic well-being. And we must spare no amount of money to prepare, to educate our next generation in the task of preparing specialists. Mandatory education is of great importance in contemporary Armenian schools. The schools of higher education, once sovereign, must establish close ties with the most advanced scientific centers of the world; and a sizable portion of students must receive their education in the best universities of other countries. The best investment of our national capital is the preparation of specialists.

With regard to defense planning, it is very probable that during the period of transition, the Soviet army currently in

---

[36] The Genocide is the second most important and widely mentioned fact by which Armenians define their ethnic identity in the diaspora (Armenia's adoption of Christianity as a state religion before anyone else in 301 A.D., is the most important, particularly in the West). In addition, the Genocide is the only event in recent history which brings all Armenians together.

The demand for the recognition of the Genocide by the international community was a major purpose of the two secret Armenian groups involved in the assassination of Turkish diplomats and attacks on Turkish targets from 1975 to 1983. See Document One, note 2.

[37] Refers to attempts by the Dashnaktsutiune-led government of the independent Armenian republic in 1920 to negotiate with Turkey as a counterbalance to Soviet Russia's pressures.

Armenia will continue to perform its strategic functions while we are permitted to develop our national army. In this respect, once it recognizes the fact of our secession, the USSR can play a major role. If, in the future, Russia wishes to maintain military bases on our territory, then that becomes subject to separate negotiations.

As far as the structure of the republic is concerned, we do not need to reinvent the wheel. We have before us the example of many other countries.

We noted the tasks that must be accomplished during the transition from semi-independent to independent status. But let us see if we will be given the possibility of becoming semi-independent. Now is the time, we have stated, to take the constitutional path toward independence, and that path will not permit the USSR leadership to use pressure against us. It does not mean that there will not be treacherous attempts to keep us away from that path. For example, there could be attempts to artificially turn the Karabagh issue into an acute crisis and to produce Armenian-Azerbaijani clashes on the border.[38] In such cases it is possible, considering the interests and possibilities of each side, to use diplomatic and military means to correct the situation. Economic pressure will not produce much result either, as was seen even in the case of Lithuania, when the blockade was obvious. All these considerations aside, we must realize that economic pressure is a weapon that can be used against us in the future, independent of our behavior. The real danger is to be expected from elsewhere.

Generally speaking, if we consider the political picture of Transcaucasia today, we note that the USSR has been able to neutralize, and make nonthreatening for itself, the popular movements in Azerbaijan and Georgia.[39] Having used the army

---

[38] In fact both predictions came true. The Armenian National Army (ANA), a group which is suspected of having close connections with the former regime and the KGB, came close to provoking a war with Azerbaijan by attacks on Azerbaijani villages. The same group was responsible for the killing of movement leader and parliament member Victor Ayvazian and his assistant when the two were approaching the ANA's headquarters to begin negotiations for the peaceful surrender of the armed groups sponsored by the group.

Neglecting Karabagh and the Azerbaijani threat was also the ostensible reason for a highly suspicious statement from the Dashnaktsutiune's Yerevan office in early September 1990. The statement called upon the armed bands to rush to the borders and guard them against imminent attack, just as a newly established government was trying to disarm the marauding bands, reestablish law and order in the city, and decrease tensions on the Azerbaijani-Armenian border.

[39] The Soviet army was used to stop a possible overthrow of the Azerbaijani government in January 1990 following the massacre of Armenians in that city.

to destroy the movement [in Azerbaijan], the USSR has bribed the general population. The greatest bribe is Artsakh.[40] Artsakh is both a bribe and a means to keep Azerbaijanis from following centrifugal tendencies. There is currently no significant movement in Azerbaijan, although no one can predict what will happen there tomorrow. The movement of Georgia is so fragmented, Moscow has so many opportunities to manipulate minority ethnic issues, and organizations functioning there are so easily given to such manipulation that Georgia too is not a source of concern for the USSR leadership.[41] The questions of ethnic minorities and the presence of autonomous regions within Georgia are providing ample opportunity for Moscow to control Georgia's centrifugal tendencies. The movement in Georgia has external luster but not depth.

The situation is different in Armenia. Our movement, being the first in the USSR, has so far kept its unity, although in the most recent period one can sense some signs of the breaking away of some forces.[42] Until very recently the important reason for the

---

The army was used to neutralize the leadership of the Azerbaijani Popular Movement, particularly its democratic and independentist wing.

[40] This is another example supporting the argument that empires tend to survive by relying on and promoting reactionary forces and that imperialism and democracy are mutually exclusive terms, at least as far as the colonies are concerned. See Document One, note 11.

[41] Ajaria, Abkhazia, and South Ossetia are autonomous regions in Georgia where Georgians are a minority. These regions have had their share of trouble, keeping the Georgian movement on a strictly nationalist, therefore vulnerable, track.

The election of Gamsakhurdia as President of Georgia strengthens the nationalist and independentist dimensions of the Georgian movement; its democratic depth will be assessed in time only.

[42] Mass demonstrations began in February 1988 and the original "Karabagh Movement Armenia Committee," or Karabagh Committee, was formed soon after. The Karabagh Committee membership was stabilized in May 1988 when the movement transcended the Karabagh issue and raised the question of democracy in Armenia. At that time three influential associates of the Committee (Zori Balayan, Sylva Kaputikian, and Igor Muratian) were left out or distanced themselves, and new forces, including Levon Ter Petrosian, joined the group.

The Karabagh Committee continued to function as the core of the Executive Committee of the Armenian National Movement (ANM) since the first Congress of the ANM in November 1990. The Committee's eleven members continued their close cooperation until the parliamentary elections ending with the victory of the ANM in August 1990. Since then, while it remains the most influential group, the Committee is less active and less apt to function as a committee. Ter Petrosian has been elected President, Manukian Prime Minister, Hambartsum Galstyan, Mayor of Yerevan, and others to various positions in parliament or the government. Some differences on issues were also bound to evolve, affecting the level of involvement of prominent members such as Rafael Ghazarian.

unity within the movement was the fact that the movement was evolving around a single hinge—the question of Artsakh. There was also another important factor, of which most of us are not deeply conscious, that strange national character which has taken root over the centuries: Our ability to achieve unity over any question of national importance, a unity that can neither be reached nor understood by others. The question of Artsakh no longer serves as the linchpin of the national movement, although the whole nation realizes the decisive importance of that question for our future and is ready to suffer greatly to see that problem resolved. And some day, when the need arises, our nation is ready to rise up as a united force in defense of our brothers and sisters [in Artsakh] against possible encroachments. To explain this [change in the centrality of the Artsakh] situation, we do not need to look for traitors and treachery.[43] There are objective reasons. The majority of our people has come to the conclusion that mass protests can no longer help; what is needed is the daily work of a few professionals, an approach on the state level. Many citizens have already understood what deep-seated problems lurk behind that question. They have also understood that rather than diverting us from the question of Artsakh, the task of strengthening our nation and our state, is on the contrary, essentially increasing our possibilities to resolve that question.

If the question of Artsakh cannot serve as the linchpin, what can?

To be enamored of economic and social reforms in an empire rushing toward its own destruction seems inane to our healthy spirited people and cannot bring our people together. To replace the Communist Party with a better national party or national parties, to replace "bad" leaders with "good" ones may be a necessary task, but that too cannot energize our people, or unite it. On the contrary, if there is no ultimate goal, that struggle can only lead to our nation's fragmentation. Should we move in

---

Under the circumstances, the Committee seems to have maintained a unique record of coherence and solidarity, a factor that continues to provide the intellectual underpinnings of the new government.

[43] The Karabagh Committee and the Armenian National Movement have come under sustained criticism from a variety of sources for having "used" the Karabagh issue to gain power and "abandoned Karabagh" since coming to power. The movement, now government, leaders have argued that the question of Karabagh cannot be resolved in and by itself and that only a strong and viable Armenia can take the issue further than where it is now. They are also taking it for granted that support for Karabagh does not mean neglect of the vital interests of the republic and its people. See note 38.

that direction, we would be spending much energy to produce few results.[44]

There is only one issue that has real possibilities, one problem whose solution will lead to the strengthening of our nation, one goal the pursuit of which will resolve the question of power in a natural way, one area where power will become a means not a purpose, one direction which will preserve our unity, one ideal around which we can expect all Armenians throughout the world to gather. That is the reestablishment of our independent statehood.[45] We ourselves may not as yet realize it strongly, but Moscow has come to comprehend that sooner or later we will reach that conclusion. That is the reason the empire considers our movement the most dangerous for itself in the Transcaucasus. Aware of this danger, Moscow prefers to give power in our republic to people who at the present are discredited even in the eyes of Moscow, profiteers from old times and otherwise unacceptable, yet supported as long as power is not turned over to the people, to the movement. The center accepts the least of two evils: Temporary power with the mandate to destroy the movement. We may complain about our lack of unity; but the unity which our people are currently displaying, and the likes of which can be found only in the Baltic republics, is frightening Moscow.[46] The possibility of striking from without, organizing Armeno-Azerbaijani clashes, or the economic pressure only help the unity of our people. This, too, is understood well in Moscow and the question of destroying the movement at any cost is part of its agenda.

[44] Unity is an issue much discussed but very little understood both in Armenia and in the diaspora. This is normal for a stateless people whose fragmentation has caused loss of power and whose lack of power has made further fragmentation possible. However, in the absence of a clearly articulated agenda agreed upon through rational debate and democratic processes, unity becomes a political tool by which one group or sides forces others to accept its agenda, solutions, mechanisms, and leadership.

[45] This articulation is critical as it integrates the question of purpose, strategy, and power. In Armenian political thinking that relied on the "third force" power and program had been treated as unrelated issues. Power in Armenia had been reduced to the question of who had access to Moscow. In the diaspora power or at least the right to speak on behalf of Armenians and make decisions in their name is claimed by organizations whose legitimacy is derived from their age (founded prior to the Genocide), participation in historical events (usually pre-1920), and survived along with the community in diaspora conditions.

The idea that power belongs to those whose program and strategy is supported by a majority of the members of the nation is being rediscovered now.

[46] This statement too runs counter to conventional Armenian wisdom which believes that Armenians are not, have not been, or could never be united.

There will be attempts, and I believe in the near future, perhaps without waiting for us to take decisive steps, to confuse the people with fabricated stories, even if for a brief period, to discredit the movement, to bring to the fore in the city armed units, armies that have been organized somehow mysteriously under the control of the authorities, to create clashes between the units, to direct the units against the movement. They may even resort to terrorism.[47] Should it become possible to destroy the movement through the use of arms, then we will witness the disappearance of the armed units (we should not delude ourselves; that is a rather easy task for the Soviet army).

To achieve all of this, it will be necessary to create antipathy against the Armenian people among all Soviets, but particularly among Russians. The Russians achieved the goal of inspiring antipathy against Azerbaijanis by organizing the massacres of Armenians in Baku. In Armenia they will reach similar goals by organizing events similar to those of May 27.[48] When one realizes what kind of confusion dominates the armed units and how they function autonomously and subjectively, it is not difficult for any chieftain with a third grade education to gather 7 to 10 armed men under him and begin to expropriate cars, extort money with impunity, and make decisions regarding the future of the nation, bringing the nation to the brink of disaster. Once these armed bands, now in Yerevan and cherished by the authorities, complete the task assigned to them (without even realizing what they are doing), that will also be their end. It is necessary to work seriously with these units, to explain what is at stake, to educate them. It is necessary to implement the decision of the Supreme Soviet to establish a security council and declare those that do not recognize the authority of that council illegal.[49] But these tasks can be achieved when our people, realizing the danger, can display decisive intolerance toward any armed individual who is found on this side of the border zone as well as toward any encroachment against the human dignity of any individual committed by

[47] The actions of the Armenian National Army and other, smaller groups from April to September 1990 confirmed this prediction.

[48] Clashes in Yerevan's railroad station between Armenians and the Soviet army provoked by the latter that resulted in 26 deaths.

[49] This is, in general terms, the strategy the author adopted when confronted with such a situation in August-September 1990 as Prime Minister of Armenia. The government was able to convince armed bands to be dissolved or join the government sponsored units on the basis of an oath of allegiance to the Parliament of Armenia.

such individuals. We must, moreover, work diligently to explain our position, our problems, and our modus operandi to the other peoples of the USSR to create a favorable public opinion.

In order to go the path of independence, we must walk the path of unity. And we will reach that unity. But there is no abstract unity. Unity is created around some noble idea, around some attainable goal. That goal, that idea, is independence.

The positing on our part of the goal of independence through constitutional methods raises a number of questions, the most difficult of which is the problem of Nakhichevan (which is conditioned by its isolated location). Without stopping to examine the various possibilities or versions of possible solution to that really complex problem, let us discuss the problem of Artsakh.

In order to understand deeply the future course of development of this issue and what we should be doing, it is necessary to understand thoroughly the political history of the whole of the previous period of the Karabagh movement. Behind the superficially obvious runarounds, petitions, strikes, massacres and resolutions passed in Moscow, Yerevan, and Baku there were hidden and complex games, to some incomprehensible; there were conflicts of interests and, occasionally, subtle diplomacy. Blows and counterblows. Numerous questions.

Was the Karabagh movement instigated or did it evolve?[50] What was the sense of pursuing the question through constitutional means when there was the obvious dead end of Article 78 of the [USSR] Constitution?[51] Why did Moscow protect Azerbaijan?[52] Did we act correctly after the Sumgait tragedy?[53] Who

---

[50] This question has been raised within the USSR as well as in the West, including some diaspora circles. In most cases the question is not raised so much to deny the legitimacy of the movement or its popular base. Rather, it may refer to the possibility of manipulation of the question once it is raised. In some instances the question is based on the assumption that all movements and causes are manipulated and masses have little political judgement.

[51] Article 78 states that no boundary changes can occur between republics without the consent of the republic adding territory as well as the one losing it. This article was in conflict with another which asserted the right of peoples for self- determination.

[52] While Armenians believe Moscow is helping Azerbaijan by not respecting their right for self-determination, Azerbaijanis believe Moscow helped the Armenian side by continuing to give Armenians reason to believe that a change in the status of Karabagh may yet occur. Both may have been correct, at least for a time. With the deployment of Soviet troops and their participation in intimidation of the population of Karabagh, the Azerbaijanis have little to complain about at this time.

[53] Sumgait, an industrial city north of the Azerbaijani capital of Baku, was

organized Sumgait and why? How do we explain the gigantic role played by the Soviet army in November 1988 in removing Armenians from Azerbaijan and Azerbaijanis from Armenia?[54] Why was the Karabagh Committee imprisoned?[55] Why was a special commission created to govern Karabagh?[56] Was the Azerbaijani blockade of Armenia an immoral act or a clever and effective step?[57] Why did the Baltic representatives vote against us when the November 28 resolution was passed at the USSR Supreme Soviet?[58] Why was a resolution proposed [in Armenia's Supreme Soviet] to declare Karabagh part of Armenia while the Karabagh Committee was in prison? Why

the site of anti-Armenian pogroms in late February and early March 1988, soon after mass demonstrations in support for self-determination of Mountainous Karabagh began in its capital Stepanakert and in Yerevan. See Samuel Shahmuratian, editor, *The Sumgait Tragedy. Eyewitness Accounts.* Volume 1. Cambridge and New York: Zoryan Institute and A. Caratzas, 1990.

54 Over 200,000 Armenians were forced to leave Armenia and some 150,000 Azeri Turks were removed from Armenia at that time. During the last three years over 300,000 Armenians have left Azerbaijan. See Document Six, note 28.

55 The December 1988 earthquake in northern Armenia was used as a cover to imprison the members and associates of the Karabagh Committee. The members of the Committee were held in Moscow for six months, without trial. They were released in June 1989, following an international campaign for their freedom and the collapse of the authority of the government in Armenia.

56 The central government appointed Arkady Volsky representative of Moscow in the Mountainous Karabagh Autonomous Region in July 1988. A special commission to govern the region was created in January 1989 under Volsky's chairmanship and the region was given a special administrative status. Volsky and the commission were dismissed some time later and locally elected authorities were dismissed. The region is currently administered by the Soviet army.

57 Azerbaijan instituted a blockade of Karabagh early in the conflict and, eventually against Armenia. The blockade was most effective in the second half of 1989. Until then 85% of all imports into Armenia had come by rail that passes through Azerbaijan. Since then, while the blockade continues to some extent, Georgia has become a more critical line of communication for Armenia. In addition to disrupting economic activities and reducing supplies in general, the blockade has created major difficulties for the earthquake reconstruction effort.

Azerbaijan's actions constituted the first-ever blockade of a republic against a region or another republic in USSR history. The central authorities' attempts at ending the blockade were perfunctory and, on occasion, contingent upon Armenians ending their struggle for self-determination.

58 The resolution, presented by President Gorbachev, dissolved the Special Commission administering Mountainous Karabagh and the region's special status, effectively reverting the region to Azerbaijani jurisdiction. Government by the Special Commission was seen by Armenians as a compromise, even if temporary, solution to the conflicting Armenian and Azerbaijani claims over the territory. The resolution received the support of 348 members of the USSR Supreme Soviet; only five voted to continue the status.

did the Karabagh Committee, from prison, oppose such a resolution? Why did the Karabagh Committee impose upon the Supreme Soviet [of Armenia] the adoption of a resolution on the creation of a united Armenia? Was the adoption of that resolution correct or incorrect? How do we explain that in the fall of 1989 the regional secretaries of the [Communist] party, the directors of factories, and the Central Committee were trying to assume the leadership of the Karabagh movement and there often was the impression promoted that the Karabagh Committee was no longer concerned with Karabagh?

All of these and other questions still await analysis and political interpretation. We need not look for complex treacheries. All these questions have simple logical answers. The important thing is that they are all tied to each other; they are not coincidences and they constitute one historical chain of events. The explanations and answers to these questions can constitute the subject of a separate article. What concerns the future course of the question, what I can say is that we must strive to fill the December 1 resolution with "meat and blood."[59] But it will still take a long time to implement that resolution. It will even be used against us. That resolution and the means to achieve it must now be considered our internal affair. To the outside world, that issue must appear in its natural dimensions: As a problem related to the right of peoples for self-determination and a human rights issue, without tying it to Armenia.[60] It is very significant for us to note that it has already been a few months that de facto, without Armenia's intervention, Artsakh has been continuing its struggle for autonomy. This demonstrates to the world, once again, that the struggle of Artsakh is an autonomous struggle for freedom based on the principles of interna-

---

[59] On December 1, 1989 the Armenian Supreme Soviet, at a joint meeting with members of the Karabagh National Council, declared the November 28, 1989 USSR Supreme Soviet resolution on Mountainous Karabagh (See previous note) null and void. Simultaneously, the joint session declared Artsakh, the historical name for Karabagh, united with Armenia and recognized the Karabagh National Council as the sole, legal authority in the region.

[60] The Karabagh Committee and the Armenian National Movement have always insisted on distinguishing between historically Armenian territories which have little or no Armenian population left, such as Nakhichevan and Western Armenia, and Karabagh, where Armenians continue to constitute the absolute majority. While claims on the first have a historical basis, self-determination is the guiding principle in the case of the latter. The principle of self-determination also distinguishes the question of Mountainous Karabagh, where the local population has been struggling to end Azerbaijani rule, and Armenian populated Akhalkalak or Javakhk in southern Georgia and bordering Armenia, where no such movement has evolved.

tional law. Those principles of international law are quite abstract; in and by themselves, they do not resolve the problem, of course, especially if there is no interested power standing behind them. But these are the principles recognized by the whole world and no state can ignore them; these principles constitute the legal and moral foundation for a given national liberation struggle. No question is resolved without a struggle, but raw power is not always sufficient to reach victory. Often a favorable public opinion plays an important role. The slogan that we must rely only on our own forces is certainly true; but it does not mean that we must isolate ourselves and artificially adopt an attitude of anger toward all. It is not wise to move from one extreme to another.[61]

Taking into consideration real feasibilities, Artsakh must be turned into an inaccessible fortress from the military point of view. We must secure within it, at the least, the current level of its national life. From the economic and political points of view, it is necessary to preserve and deepen its autonomy, taking into view the fact that the direction toward which the USSR is currently headed may be propitious for the solution of that problem (with some caution, it is also possible to benefit from the contradictions emerging in Moscow).

We must also resist the blackmail from Moscow, which tries to tie our independence to the question of Karabagh. To increase our possibilities to resolve that problem we must declare independence and continue in a state of transitional semi-independence while waiting for an appropriate moment for the solution of the problem. We can see no prospect of resolving the Karabagh issue as long as we remain within the structure of the USSR.

Speaking of the guarantees of independent statehood, there is, naturally, a question raised regarding the fact that Turkey is our neighbor. In a previous section, we discussed the possibility of a threat from Turkey in the case of a Soviet collapse; we stated that, deviating for a moment from its current policy of development, Turkey may try to absorb some easily digestible parts of the collapsing empire. That possibility is one of the important reasons for our proposing and pressing toward a declaration of independence before such a dangerous moment arises. Everyone agrees easily that Turkey may try to absorb some pieces of the empire. But not everyone agrees that Turkey has

---

[61] The reference is mainly to the position advocated by Paruyr Hayrikian and his organization. See Document One, notes 69-71.

opted for a path of internal development which makes feasible, during a time of peace, the coexistence of Armenia and Turkey.

The example of Cyprus is always brought in. Rather than examine the question of Cyprus directly, I prefer to offer numerous proofs, leaving it to the reader to assess those proofs. Let us note, nonetheless, that the peaceful coexistence of neighboring countries is not guaranteed solely by the decision taken by each in favor of development, nor by the restraints forced on the other by the presence of military power, but also by international responsibilities, by the interests of many countries to keep a balance of power. Conquests become possible when, in some way or another, the chain of international responsibilities is broken, when an unstable situation is created in a region, when there are revolutions and upheavals, when the definition of interests of other countries changes, and when there are more or less adequate bases for the introduction of military forces.[62] In this respect, one can say that just about all independent countries are in the same predicament; the existence of each is secured by military force, by the politics that is led, by international responsibilities, and by the stability of the region. Let us now look at the facts dealing with the history of Cyprus.

Cyprus has been a British colony since 1924.[63] In 1955 began the struggle for national liberation to create an independent republic. In 1959 the three interested countries, England, Turkey, and Greece signed the Zurich-London agreements, according to which the three countries assumed the role of guarantors for the independence of Cyprus, recognizing its right to an independent existence. According to these agreements, England obtained the right to have military bases, while Turkey and Greece were permitted to keep army units on the island. In 1960 Cyprus adopted a constitution according to which the president of the country had to be of Greek origin and the vice president of Turkish origin; similarly, the parliament was to be made up of 35 Greek and 15 Turkish elected members. In 1963 there were clashes between the two communities, following which the Turks refused to participate in parliamentary and governmental institutions. In 1967 the Turks created their own executive administration. In 1974 relations between Turkey and Greece

[62] The case of Iraq's invasion of Kuwait and the international response may provide arguments to both sides.

[63] The Ottoman Empire turned over administration of Cyprus to the British in 1878, in return for British protection of the Ottomans against Russia following the signing of the Treaty of San Stefano. See Document One, note 18. But the island state became a British crown colony only in 1924.

deteriorated due to the question of control over the oil reserves found in the Aegean Sea. In 1974 the Greek military in the island's army raised the flag of revolt against the legitimate government by demanding that the island be annexed to Greece. This was followed by the invasion of Turkish forces on the island, which occupied 40% of the island's territory during the months of July and August. There was a rare coincidence of interests regarding this invasion between the forces of NATO and the USSR. No one intervened. There were only formal protests aimed at quieting the public opinion. In July 1974, the military junta left power in Greece and was replaced by the government of C. Karamanlis. On August 14 his government declared its intention to leave the military structure of NATO. In February 1975 the Turkish sector of Cyprus made a unilateral declaration regarding the creation of a federative republic in Cyprus. Currently the Turkish part of Cyprus is not annexed to Turkey; rather an independent republic has been declared on that territory, recognized only by Turkey. There are intense negotiations among the interested parties regarding the question of Cyprus. Events in the USSR are now likely to decrease the importance of Turkey for NATO and many are hopeful that sooner or later, a unified government will reassert its authority over the whole island.

One other question related to independence is troubling our people a good deal. How will we go about the reunification of [Western Armenian] territories occupied by Turkey and now practically devoid of any Armenian population? As an independent country, will we not be weaker than Turkey in practically every area? I do not have an answer; if someone can propose a feasible program to obtain the reunification of our lands I am sure we will support it, the whole nation will support it, and we will spare neither life nor energy to make it happen. But I know one thing for certain. Hopes according to which Russia will one day return to its imperialistic policies, that it will have the opportunity to occupy those lands, that it will then return them to us and then disappear, giving us the chance to have a united and independent Armenia, are altogether baseless;[64] [these hopes] lead our people to idleness and slavery, condemning us to disappear from the face of the earth as a nation. Equally baseless are those hopes that a recognition of

---

[64] The "unification of lands first, independence later" formula summarizes the position of some groups within Armenia and the most important of the diaspora political organizations, the Dashnaktsutiune, during the last few years. See Appendix B2.

the Genocide by the United Nations may lead to a return of our lands to us, although such a recognition does have significance for our people.

The only hope I see now is that the unpredictable ups and downs of history may provide us with an opportunity to resolve the territorial issues we must face as an independent nation, a state, and not as an ethnic unit in the process of being assimilated in Russia. It does not mean, of course, that we must forget our territorial demands; what it does mean is that territorial demands cannot constitute for us at this time a national or state policy. Those demands must constitute the unifying factor for various public organizations, compatriotic unions; they must always be alive in the memory of our people and be our youthful dream until such time as opportunities are created to resolve those problems[65] [. . .]

The British say that they have two powerful weapons: Nuclear bombs and democracy. We do not have the first and we are not availing ourselves of the second. It is time that our historians and our writers abstain from the constant wailing that weakens our people and from mentioning the tragic pages alone. We were once powerful and will be so again. We have been at one time considered the best soldiers of the East,[66] we have given the world an unparalleled architecture.[67] After the loss of our statehood and through the peaceful means of commerce, we have represented tremendous weight in India and China. In the British Parliament deputies argued that without dealing with Armenians it is impossible to conquer India.[68] We have been at the root of reformation, which transformed Europe and which

---

[65] The words used here to relegate the question of territorial claims against Turkey to the distant future are practically the same as those used by Dashnaktsutiune leader Hrair Marukhian to turn independence into a vision having little to do with real politics. See Appendix B2.

[66] This must be a reference to Urartuan (ninth-sixth centuries B.C.), Artashesian (second-first Centuries B.C.) and Bagratuni (ninth to tenth centuries A.D.) periods.

[67] Claims based on the writings of Austrian art historian Josef Strzhigowski (1862-1941), especially his *Die Bakunst Der Armenier und Europa*. Vienna, 1918.

[68] Refers to inroads made by Armenian merchants in the India trade in the seventeenth century, leading to the agreement between the British East India Company and the association of Armenian merchants in 1686. This agreement gave Armenians extensive prerogatives in trade in India but imposed a British monopoly on transportation of products. Such an agreement became necessary for the British because Indian rulers allowed the stateless and harmless Armenians to develop trade, while British traders were considered a prelude to complete British domination. Once intermediaries became unnecessary, the British forced Armenians to limit their activities in size and scope. See Document One, note 11.

led to the development of our contemporary civilization.[69] God has kept us and led us through millennia of temptations and all of that has not been done in order for us now to condemn our nation to oblivion because of our idleness and indecisiveness [...] Those who are afraid and weak can leave the homeland. They are the dust of the nation.[70] Let the strong remain; those who are striving to live with dignity in their own homeland; those who have faith in the future of our nation; those who are Armenian by their essence; those who think Armenian, leaning on our history, our land, and our water. And shoulder to shoulder, we will rebuild our former strength, our state.

[69] Probably a reference to the Paulician and Thondrakian social-religious movements (seventh-eleventh centuries) which, in the view of some, inspired European Protestantism.

[70] Reference to the sustained emigration from Armenia during the last two decades. Under Brezhnev, emigration was permitted for those Armenians and their relatives who had immigrated from the diaspora largely following the Second World War. In conjunction with the international human rights campaign to allow Soviet Jews to leave the USSR, that right was extended by Soviet authorities to Armenians and Germans as well, although diaspora Armenian organizations neither demanded nor supported Armenian emigration.

Document Five

Interview With Ktrich Sardarian

This interview preceded the adoption of the Declaration on Independence by the Parliament of Armenia. First published in Hayk *(August 24, 1990), it asserts the right of the democratically elected Parliament to develop foreign and domestic policies which will help build a viable, self-reliant nation- state. In large measure, it is a response to criticisms of the Armenian National Movement, as friends and antagonists alike realized that the new government may, in fact, adopt policies based on the principles for which the democratic movement stood.*

A historian by training, Ktrich Sardarian was elected to the Parliament during the May 1990 elections and was soon elected chairman of the important Committee on Independent Statehood and National Policy. More recently, he was called upon to serve as Vice-Prime Minister.

The interview was conducted by Arthur Andranikian.

Question: *Mr. Sardarian, the Committee on Independent Statehood and National Policy[1] has now taken shape. Could you tell us a few words about the task it will be undertaking?*

As you know, within a few days, the Parliament will be adopting the Declaration on Independence, which will give Armenia a new status.[2] This marks the beginning of a qualitatively new period in Armenian history. Parliament decided to establish a standing committee whose essential task it is to assure the unhindered development of the process of independence that is just under way and to see that process through.

[1] One of seventeen standing Committees of the Parliament.

[2] A Declaration on Independence was, in fact, adopted the day this interview appeared, on August 24, 1990. See Document Seven.

Let me first define my understanding of independence. As you know, there was quite a debate in Parliament on the Declaration on Independence. Many were insisting that it is necessary to relate [in that declaration] our [nation's] biography and, particularly, to declare null and void those treaties that were signed at our expense.³ These treaties are our history, our biography, which have no yield in today's political world. It is possible to go a step further and say that including these treaties may complicate our activities in the future. We must act politically and be practical. We must adopt documents we have the power and ability to realize. In this respect I believe our Committee must be circumspect, it must not burden itself with wish lists, and it must distinguish between wish and feasibility. Politics is power and feasibility.

Today we have a historical feasibility of taking a step, to begin the process of independence. If today we adopt documents whose contents, however just historically, we have no power and ability to execute, we will have destroyed the authority of our newly elected parliament. Here too it is one of the tasks of the Committee to ensure that the laws and legislative acts which the Parliament will be adopting on the basis of the principles enunciated in the declaration are politically circumspect. This consideration is one aspect of the work of the Committee. The other concern is to ensure that in our actions we are led strictly by our national interests. What I am suggesting is that the path to the resolution of our main issue, to the achievement of our visions passes through the establishment of a nation state.⁴ If we are able to create an independent and strong state, I believe new doors will be open for our nation. Should we be unable to achieve this, the rest become mere wishes with which you can do nothing in politics.

When we are currently in the process of laying the cornerstone of our statehood, we should not be hasty. We have a historic opportunity to erect the structure of our state, setting stone

---

3 These are the treaties of Kars and Moscow signed in 1921 between Soviet Russia, acting on behalf of Armenia as well, and Turkey. These treaties leave intact the provisions of the Treaty of Alexandrapol (Leninakan, now Gumayri) signed under duress by the the government of the Republic of Armenia on December 2, 1920, according to which Western Armenian territories, including once Russian-occupied Kars and Artahan, would revert to Turkish jurisdiction.

4 The assertion that independence is a feasible goal while territorial unification is relegated to the future is in agreement with the approach of other members of the Armenian National Movement. It is in direct conflict with the generally accepted wisdom within politically active groups mainly in the diaspora which, after much meandering, had reached the opposite conclusion.

upon stone. If we deviate from that goal, if we take uncircumspect steps, inevitably we will have set our neighbors against us, because declaring those treaties null and void will lead us exactly there. Whether people realize it or not, wittingly or unwittingly, that would be the result. It is completely incomprehensible to me what we will have achieved if our Parliament declared the March 16, 1921 Russo-Turkish treaty void. What will we have attained, practically speaking? For me politics has a practical significance. If [declaring that treaty void] gives us something in concrete terms, let us do it; if not, it will be a wasted act.

Question: In fact, the Committee will be concerned with the reestablishment of national statehood. Don't you consider it among your tasks to unmask those Bolsheviks who labored to strengthen the Russo-Turkish solidarity, as a result of which the remaining piece of Armenia bled to death? I have in mind in particular Atabekyan,[5] Avis,[6] Karakhan,[7] and others. There is known evidence that at Lenin's request Leo Karakhan hid Enver[8] in his Moscow house. I repeat. Don't you think it necessary that in the process of nation building such traitors be unmasked?

For me history, the mention of history, the pages of history in the political context have only a moral significance. It is known, however, that moral arguments alone achieve little in politics. Politics is, first of all, power, and circumspect calculation. We can become a state only when we think in realistic terms. I view the revealing of historical pages in the following context. Our generations must see for themselves where we have gone wrong; for example: in what sense the actions of the Bol-

---

[5] Levon N. Atabekian, an Armenian Bolshevik activist (1875- 1918).

[6] Avis Nourijanian, Bolshevik activist, one of the signers of the Sovietization treaty (1896-1937).

[7] Leo or Lev Karakhan, Bolshevik activist and diplomat who worked in the Soviet Russian Foreign Ministry; he was one of the negotiators with Turkey (1889-1937).

[8] One of the leaders of the Young Turk movement, Enver Pasha (1881-1922) organized, along with Talaat and Jemal Pashas, the 1913 coup that concentrated power in the hands of the triumvirate. Enver was Minister of the Navy of the Ottoman Empire during the First World War and is one of the Turkish leaders responsible for the planning and implementation of the Genocide of Armenians. Enver fled to Russia after the collapse of the Ottoman Empire and attempted to use the Pan-Islamic and Pan-Turkic ideologies to create a new base of power in Central Asia after the collapse of the Ottoman Empire. See also Document One, note 43.

sheviks constitute treason. There are already some writings on that subject, there should be more in-depth treatment in that respect.

Question: You will excuse me, but how about the accentuated anti-nationalism . . .

It is simple and natural. That too. The international revolution was directed fully against the Armenian state, and it is natural that their activities must be considered acts of treason. But they were tools in the hands of their party. Working in the Ministry of Foreign Affairs of Russia, Karakhan was implementing directives received from Moscow. He is also tied to Enver. In autumn of 1920 Enver was in Moscow. The Soviet government was doing everything possible to reconcile Enver and Kemal.[9] The President of Armenia's delegation, Levon Shant,[10] has many references to the flirtation between Enver and Moscow. At the time Moscow had become a peculiar Mecca for political activists. Special divisions were being formed to be placed under Enver's disposition.

One of the tasks of the committee will be to reveal all the pages, particularly those that may be considered critical, of history, so that the new generation does not make the same mistakes, so that it has the consciousness of this land, of being master of the fatherland. We must help history serve politics, we must learn from the past. We must ensure that the Armenian is dedicated to this soil and water, so that he stops putting his neck under someone else's yoke. It is really a monumental task related to our whole system of education and to changes in other fields. We will, of course, pay attention to these related matters. We must develop programs dealing with political direction, programs that will help us and serve the goal of establishing relations with our neighbors.

---

[9] Kemal is Mustafa Kemal or Kemal Ataturk (1881-1938), considered founder of the Republic of Turkey in 1923 and modernizer of the state. Following the Ottoman defeat in the First World War, Kemal organized and led the War of Independence.

[10] Levon Shant, born Seghbosian (1869-1951) was a writer of Western Armenian origin who became a leading member of the Dashnaktsutiune-led government of the Republic of Armenia from 1918 to 1920.

Shant chaired the Parliament and in the summer of 1920 headed the Armenian delegation that negotiated with Soviet Russia.

Question: You mentioned that relations must be established with neighboring countries. How do you think these negotiations should be conducted in view of historical issues?[11]

One can always note a contradiction here. For twenty years or so I have studied the issues of Armenian history and particularly the period 1918-1921. These issues are more complex and weightier than assumed. Today there is a universal focus on the history of that period because there is hunger for the historical mind and not all pages of that history are revealed.

Particularly for the younger generation, it seems that by making noise again, by petitioning and by appealing to international forums, and by constantly talking about the justice of the Armenian claims will we achieve something.[12] It is true there is evidence that the world is civilized, that the UN itself has changed. But still, I will repeat, since politics is interest and calculation, civilized man calculates better. Those international bodies and, during 1919-1923 the League of Nations, said some wonderful things about the Armenian people, greeted the establishment of the Armenian state. But when Turkey attacked Armenia [1921] no one lifted a finger to help. History, then, is teaching us some lessons in this respect. When it comes to politics, we should never place our hopes on the foreigner. If we do not begin to rely on our own strength, if we are not circumspect—while, of course, cooperating with all these forces—and if we think that the UN or the European Parliament may help Armenians only because our cause is just, we will have been mistaken fundamentally. You must conquer your right yourself. The moment of recognition will follow. It is very important for us to become a subject of international law.

It is important that we create stability within our republic.[13] [. . .] We must be able to stabilize the situation and prove as a

---

[11] Reference to willingness of the present government to develop relations with Turkey considering the Genocide, the non- recognition of the Genocide by republican Turkey, the claims Armenians have on Western Armenian (Eastern Turkish) provinces, and the array of resentments and negative feelings which permeate every aspect of Armenian-Turkish relations.

[12] Tactics prevalent in the diaspora and sometimes regarded with wonder in Armenia mainly demonstrative acts that attract attention, meetings with representatives of foreign governments, and campaigns for the recognition of the Genocide by international bodies such as the UN.

[13] Refers to the multiplication of volunteer armed units originally created to defend Armenian lives at the Azerbaijani-Armenian border. Some returned to the cities and caused lawlessness and the problem of the "armed brigades" terrorizing the civilian population. Had it not been resolved soon, the problem

state that the only path to salvation is the development of the state, that through partisan fighting and the *fedayee* psychology[14] we have achieved nothing and will achieve nothing. Witness the current events.

Now we are creating special units attached to the Ministry of Internal Affairs that will include all the patriotic forces. If the latter have armed themselves to defend their fatherland, the must obey their government. I fail to understand those forces who wish to spread chaos and anarchy in Armenia. Of course this view is not merely an assessment of the actions of armed brigades but also of those of their sponsors. It is clear that they are backed by elements who are unwilling to reconcile with the democratic changes sweeping the country, and with the idea that the people have now initiated the process of independent statehood.[15] These elements are not interested in those goals at all. They may be making speeches to the contrary but their actions, their politics will destroy our nation. The forces that are deepening the chaos in our country are working directly against our newly created state.

I am in favor of a normal course of action in affairs of state.

Question: Are you referring to independence by phases?

Yes. You know that independence is a relative concept. For me independence is not a purpose in itself. It is my deep belief that independence is necessary for the moral development of our people, since there is no moral development outside independent statehood; otherwise the nation can survive, drag its existence in a slavish state, just as it did during the last 70 years. The people must either live free or not live. Existence as a slave nation is truly intolerable for nations that have dignity. But it does not mean that we must switch from one extreme situation to another.

---

would have threatened the new government's stability and credibility, while providing the Kremlin an excuse to intervene militarily. See also Document Four, note 47.

[14] *"Fedayee"* is a term used for the guerrilla fighter in the liberation movement against the Ottoman Empire at the end of the nineteenth and early twentieth century largely under the leadership of the political parties now in the diaspora. The *fedayee*'s main attributes were his courage and his spirit of devotion and martyrdom meant to assert Armenian rights and a new identity rather than the execution of a strategy with well defined political and military goals.

[15] The reference is largely to the Communist Party and its constituents.

Question: To be honest, I had a sense that our conversation would be more on history. As you noted earlier, the invalidation of treaties is untimely. There is much talk recently about the Treaty of Sevres.16 For me that treaty is a moral treaty. Would you please tell us something regarding our position on that treaty?

The Treaty of Sevres guarantees, of course, the territorial integrity of the Republic of Armenia [1918-1920]—only on paper. But I have already stated that in politics nothing is achieved by mere moral arguments. A few days ago, some pathetic appeals were made for the immediate implementation of the [provisions of] the Treaty of Sevres. It is easy to use the word "immediate." But how? Turkey is a powerful country. Do we want today to create a state on the territory we have or do we want to dwell on wishes . . .? If you put on your shoulders weight heavier than you can carry, you achieve nothing.

Question: Diasporan parties often present claims and propose "unification of land" and "unification of nation" as purposes . . .17

First of all I do not understand what these terms, "unification of land" and "unification of people" mean. These are bombastic words, incomprehensible to me. Of course it is our hallowed dream to see all Armenian territories reunited. But it is clear that many forces are exploiting our national dreams for political purposes [. . .] Let us leave that aside. For me, now more than ever, it is the political situation that counts.

[16] See Document One, note 45.

[17] The Armenian words are *azgahavak* (literally "gathering of the nation") and *hoghahavak* ("gathering of the lands"). Reference mainly to the Dashnaktsutiune whose goal of Free, Independent and United Armenia was recently turned into the slogan encompassing these two words. By unification of lands the Dashnaktsutiune has in mind Mountainous Karabagh and Nakhichevan (in Azerbaijan), Akhalkalak (in Georgia), and Western Armenian territories (in Turkey). Unification of the people refers to the return of all diaspora Armenians to the unified lands.

By giving priority to these two goals—and considering them feasible—the current leadership of the Dashnaktsutiune is arguing that independence is neither feasible nor desirable, since the first two cannot be accomplished without a state that has the power to take on Turkey, namely the USSR or Russia or, in Rafael Ishkhanian's more generic term, the "third force." The ideal of a free Armenia too has suffered in recent statements from the party. The underlying assumption is that if we need the USSR to help us realize the unification of lands, we cannot afford a government that may not do Kremlin's bidding. See Appendix C1, note 4.

In Parliament they talk a lot about confederation and federation. Yet the process of independence has gripped the whole of the empire. The empire is disintegrating. What shape will it have tomorrow? One thing is evident. Russia is already convinced that by oppressing others, it is distorting the moral character of its own people. And since the process has started, one should make certain that we are not under the rubble when the structure collapses. . . Remember Isahakian's[18] characteristic statement in 1920: What collapsed at the turn of the century, collapsed over the head of our people. For me circumspection and caution are the hinges of our political positioning. In fact, in an anarchic situation such as we have, I do not find it useful to discuss political independence. Of course, we can declare such an independence tomorrow, and no one will stop us. Although I do not like comparisons, let us look at the Lithuanian version and our own process. Lithuania declared its independence. But [independence] requires more than a declaration. Lithuania was unable to get international recognition because developments in the USSR are such that Gorbachev has become an international player. No major power—it is obvious that the UN is an organization of major powers and not one that pursues just causes—has recognized Lithuania's independence. For that reason Lithuania "froze" its Declaration of Independence and the process is only beginning.

By our own process, we will prove to our people that the creation of independent national statehood is the only path to salvation . . .

[18] See Document One, note 25.

Document Six

Statement of Levon Ter Petrosian Armenian National Movement Candidate for the Presidency of the Armenian Supreme Soviet

This statement was presented as the campaign "platform" of the movement's candidate for the presidency of the Supreme Soviet—effectively, of the republic. The statement summarizes past and current experiences, lessons learned and ideals adopted, to present one argument: To solve its problems and live in dignity, Armenia must become a free and sovereign state. The concerns and principles articulated here will also inform the new Parliament's Declaration on Independence, which was to follow Ter Petrosian's election, both in August 1990.

Ter Petrosian was elected on the fourth ballot competing against the candidate of the Communist Party, then First Secretary of the Armenian CP Vladimir Movsesian. While the democratic coalition led by the Armenian National Movement had won a majority of the seats in the new Parliament, the absolute majority needed for victory was achieved with the defection of Communist members. The latter were concerned that the Communist Party had lost all authority and credibility and only an ANM supported candidate could have the popular support to prevent a civil war.

Levon Ter Petrosian is a philologist-historian. Until he joined the Karabagh Committee in May 1988, and for a short time after, he was senior researcher at the Matenadaran, the main repository of Armenian manuscripts in Yerevan, and lecturer at the Gevorgian Seminary of Echmiadsin.

The text of his statement was first disseminated by Armenpress on August 10, 1990 and widely reprinted in the Armenian press.

Honorable Chairman, Honorable Members:

Allow me to begin by cautioning you that my presentation will be better characterized as a political statement rather than a program. It is dictated by the critical situation in the USSR and in our republic.

The general direction of the course of events in the USSR and the experience of the Armenian people, from the perspective of the Republic of Armenia,[1] are signaling major political developments characterized by the following:

1. Independent national statehood based on a sovereign economic program;

2. A government of law[2] based on the norms established by international law;

3. A democratic system anchored in universal values and human rights.

If we compare the concrete points adopted by some of the Soviet republics in their declarations of independence or sovereignty, we will note that, except for some details, they are very much alike in their essence. Almost all republics emphasize the following steps as having priority within their national programs:

1. The development of a sovereign economic program;
2. Control of their own national wealth;
3. Strengthening of interrepublican cooperation and the internal market;
4. Application of independent tax policies and monetary systems;
5. Diversity of modes of property ownership;
6. Radical revision of obligations formulated with regard to the Union;
7. Ensuring the supremacy of the republic's constitution and laws;
8. Establishment of direct relations with foreign countries;
9. Creation of their own military and security forces;
10. Separation of executive, legislative, and judiciary powers;[3]

---

[1] First use of the term "Republic of Armenia" as opposed to Soviet Armenia or Armenian SSR. The name was to be changed officially with the Declaration on Independence on August 23, 1990.

[2] The term "government of law" is the more commonly used in English, while the Armenian term is closer to the French "state," or *etat*, of law.

[3] In the original, the term used is "branches."

11. Depoliticization of state institutions;
12. Privatization of social life;[4]
13. Establishment of a multi-party system and of full democratic freedoms;
14. Security of development of national language, culture, etc.

I am sure that the same picture will be projected in the legislative proposals to be offered by all political groups, including the Communist Party, since that is the objective imperative of development in the USSR today. All the republics, sooner or later, will be adopting this path of sovereignty and democracy. It seems that with some reservations, the central authorities will be obligated to reconcile with this tendency.

In this case it is possible to raise the question: What are the specific principles, articulated within the national program of each republic, that must be considered basic and which will allow people to orient themselves and make choices?

In my opinion, there are two such objective principles.

The first is related to the stand with regard to the new agreement on the Union or with regard to federation.[5]

The second is related to the emergence of forces that are in a position to execute the national agenda.

With regard to the first principle, we must realize that the tendency within the Union to limit the powers of the Union government and to increase the powers of the republics and autonomous units is an essential one. On the one hand, we have the central authorities who, in words, insist on the need to create a more perfect Soviet federation but whose legislation aims at the preservation of the totalitarian basis of government within the country. On the other hand, we have the republics and autonomous units that are trying to establish their sovereignty and, as a general rule, are standing in opposition to the central constitution and the system of laws governing the Union.

Political thinking in the country offers three solutions to this contradiction: The signing of a new Union agreement, the replacement of the [single, unitary] agreement with bilateral agreements between republics, or a combination of the two.

---

[4] The "social" sphere refers to the arts, culture, entertainment, etc. The word "political" in Eastern Armenian is *"hasarakakan,"* which translated literally, means "public."

[5] A federation of republics proposed by USSR President Mikhail Gorbachev instead of the current union. The proposal seems to have come too late and offered too little to interest the republics with centrifugal tendencies. See Document Nine for Ter Petrosian's analysis of the state of the Union.

Considering the integrating forces at work within the world, and by realistically assessing historically defined realities, it is impossible to exclude any one of the three possibilities.

It is clear that the Republic of Armenia, without having to wait for the final solution of the question and considering its own national interests must, even today, sign bilateral economic and political agreements with all the republics and autonomous units in the Union.

A Union agreement may be acceptable within the foreseeable future only if the following conditions are fulfilled:

1. Armenia participates in that agreement as an entity that has standing under international law;

2. There will be no attempts to apply the Union constitution and Union laws on the territory of Armenia.

It is not difficult to foresee that one of the most serious issues raised by a Union agreement is the determination of the status of the Soviet army. Currently all republics, including Russia, are leaning toward the idea of the creation of national armed units. The fulfilling of draft obligations by all soldiers in their own republic is thus seen as the first step in that direction. It appears that the future possibility of the temporary presence on republic territories of Soviet or Russian military units—whose presence is regulated by international treaties—is not excluded.

By noting these tendencies suggested by the objective course of events, it is also necessary to underline that such a radical revision of mutual responsibilities between republics and the Union requires of the parties the display of a high level of appreciation of partnership relations; of realistic approaches; and of the willingness to seek solely political solutions, avoiding recourse to arms, to undesirable confrontations and the unnecessary sharpening of conflicts.

As to the phases we must go through to achieve the reestablishment of national statehood, that hardly depends on the whim of individuals or on the proposals of political parties. Rather, it depends on the attitude of the Parliament, which reflects the people's will in concrete situations and, when needed, on the verdict of a general popular referendum.

One thing is clear, as shown by the example of Lithuania. Independence is not accomplished by a singular act; it is accomplished through a process that requires a monumental system of specific acts executed systematically over a period of time.[6]

---

[6] The statement presages the flexibility that was to be reflected in the Declaration on Independence on August 24, 1990.

This brings us to the second question: Which political forces can execute these steps and create the political, economic, legal, and spiritual preconditions for the sovereign and independent existence of the Republic of Armenia? Here, we must take into consideration the fact that, in addition to the problems it shares with other republics, Armenia has those that are unique to it: The question of Artsakh, the reconstruction of the disaster zone, and the instability caused by the presence of armed bands are issues that further complicate the historic mission of the next government.[7]

Unlike other republics that have taken the path of sovereignty or independence such as the Baltics, Russia, the Ukraine, and Moldavia, here in Armenia the levers of power are still in the hands of the upper echelons of the Communist Party. It seems the Communist Party has no intention at this time of giving up those levels or to share them with the newly emerged democratic forces—and thus sharing responsibility with the people. The proof is in the ferocious electoral campaign waged by the Communist Party apparatus in its illegal and antidemocratic behavior during the current session, as testified amply by the attempts of the *apparat* to lay siege to the commission examining the credentials of delegates; and in its reluctance to call into account those electoral commissions that had allowed irregularities.[8]

Under the circumstances, is it possible to trust the fate of the Armenian people once again to a party whose 70 years of culpable life has brought the republic to the brink of destruction? That party, created by foreigners and serving foreigners, has no relation to our national aspirations and goals. It was that party which, with the intervention of external forces, brought to an end the Republic of Armenia, in the name of the victory of international revolution,[9] by giving more than half of the

---

[7] See Document Four, note 47, and Document Five, note 13.

[8] Irregularities included the withholding of papers necessary for registration of Armenian National Movement and other non-Communist candidates, provocative and violent acts falsely blamed on the democratic forces, intimidation, etc.

[9] Refers to the Sovietization of Armenia in December 1920. According to official Soviet historiography, it was achieved by a "socialist revolution" from within by Armenia's Bolsheviks. In fact it was forced by the Red Army upon an Armenia facing the Nationalist Army of Turkey to the West.
The role of Armenian Bolsheviks must be assessed on a number of levels. Historically they became the "fig leaf" for the invading Russian forces. Armenian Bolsheviks themselves were convinced that the Russian Revolution—harbinger of the world revolution—and the establishment of Soviet rule were the best guarantees for the solution of the Armenian Question.

republic to Turkey and Azerbaijan.[10] It destroyed the lifestyle of the village by expropriating the peasant;[11] it organized the massive murders and persecutions of 1937 and 1949.[12]

Some may argue that all of that belongs to the past and that the Party of the era of perestroika has nothing to do with these crimes. Such an objection would have been appropriate and justified only if after the beginning of the liberation struggle in February 1988 the Party had provided assurances of serving the interests of our people.[13]

Instead of leading the powerful democratic movement, for two and one half years the Communist Party of Armenia acted as a fifth column for Moscow, obstructing all political initiatives coming from below. And it was only under the tremendous pressure created by the masses and under duress that it acquiesced to the expansion of sovereign rights, to the process of democratization, and to the solution of the question of Artsakh. Let us remember with what vehemence the official authorities of the republic opposed the June 15, 1989, and December 1, 1989, resolutions concerning the reunification of Artsakh,[14] the decree relating to democratization; the demands concerning the protection of the environment, etc.[15]

[10] Territorial disputes were solved during or immediately after the Sovietization of Armenia, usually at the expense of Armenia. Mountainous Karabagh and Nakhichevan were awarded to Azerbaijan; the treaties of Kars and Moscow confirmed the Treaty of Alexandrapol and Turkish control over Western Armenia. See Document Five, note 3.

[11] Much of rural Armenia, and USSR, was destroyed during the mass expropriation of land and cattle in the late 1920s and early 1930s.

[12] Most of the Armenian intelligentsia was decimated during the Great Purges executed by Stalin and Beria during 1936-1939. A lesser known wave was unleashed in 1949 against those suspected of "nationalism," "anti-socialism," etc. This wave included a large number of Armenians from the diaspora who had just repatriated in 1945-1947.

[13] February 1988 marks the beginning of the new phase of the struggle. It was on February 20 that the Regional Soviet of Mountainous Karabagh passed a resolution demanding reunification with Armenia. Mass demonstrations in support of the resolution in Stepanakert and Yerevan followed.

[14] See Document Four, notes 58 and 59.

[15] The most prominent of the demands with regard to the environment were the closing of (a) the Medsamor nuclear energy plant near Yerevan and (b) the Nayirit rubber factories within city limits. Both were recognized as serious health hazards before the eruption of the Karabagh issue. In fact the first public demonstrations, in the fall of 1987, were against the absence of environmental policies, of the government.

The earthquake of December 1988 refocused attention on the potential danger of accidents at either one of those plants. Both plants were shut down eventu-

Let us not forget also that it was the same authorities that dissolved the local branches of the Karabagh Committee in March 1988 by presidential decree; who in December 1988 introduced the military curfew in Yerevan and parts of Armenia; who imprisoned the members of the Karabagh Committee and the various activists of the movement; who flooded the mass media with charges taken out of the 1937 armory, etc.[16] This is the real picture of the bureaucracy of the Communist Party in the era of perestroika, of what it believes to maintain power, and of its claim to achieve the goals of the Armenian people.

As long as the Communist Party of Armenia is tied to the Communist Party of the USSR on the basis of the principle of centralization and is governed from without, it cannot serve the interests of the Armenian people and it cannot be trusted to resolve the critical problems our people are facing. Only when it cuts off its subjective relations with the Communist Party of the USSR can it become a national party and make a significant contribution to the task of realizing our national aspirations. It does not mean that the representatives of the Communist Party and its rank and file are not part of the process of national liberation. We appreciate their role in this struggle as well as their weighty political experience and organizational and administrative abilities. We are certain that all the healthy elements of the party, regardless of political and subsequent changes, will perform their duty toward the fatherland and nation selflessly.

---

ally, although all recognized that the first would produce energy shortages and the second would take away approximately 10,000 jobs and a major export in an already depressed economy. Moscow was opposed to the closing of both, particularly of Nayirit, which served the whole of the USSR and Eastern Europe. Some believe that the cutting off of the natural gas pipeline into Armenia in late 1990 was a punitive measure taken by Moscow in retaliation for the closing of Nayirit.

The new government has stated that Medsamor may be temporarily reopened if Armenia loses other sources of energy and Nayirit may be reopened if appropriate filters are found and installed.

[16] The anti-Movement campaign was facilitated by the attention to the earthquake that struck the northern third of the republic on December 8, 1988. The government used the spontaneous support shown the authorities by individuals, organizations and governments outside Armenia to settle its accounts with the democratic movement. The curfew and imprisonment of the members of the Karabagh Committee members was facilitated by the attitude of Mikhail Gorbachev who chided Armenians for thinking "politics" instead of helping their brethren.

The politicization of the earthquake was inevitable, given the paralysis of the government in the face of the disaster as contrasted with the ability of the movement to organize effective aid with popular support.

With regard to the other political forces within the republic,[17] who today raise the serious issue of sharing responsibility in the making of the future of the Armenian people, I feel obligated to note the following.

Two or three years after the announcement of the policies of perestroika and glasnost,[18] the peoples of the USSR were convinced that the party and the economic bureaucracy of the country was in no position to execute the announced policy. Moreover, that bureaucracy was creating obstacles to the realization of centrally proposed moderate steps toward democratization and the tentative and fearful attempts at autonomy for republics. For that reason, there emerged in different parts of the country, in a powerful surge, many political organizations, associations, and groups that were not only transformed into widely based social movements but also became—if not an opposition—at least an alternative, people-based authority.[19] And in a very short period of time these movements achieved much more concrete results in the areas of democratization and sovereignty of peoples than it was possible to achieve during the three preceding years, when [democratization and sovereignty came] in the form of charity doled out by the central authorities.

The national liberation struggle of the Armenian people was one of those powerful social movements which, under extremely unfavorable conditions and persecutions, achieved the following palpable results.

    1.   The June 15 and December 1, 1989 resolutions of Armenia's Supreme Soviet concerning the reunification of Artsakh and Armenia;

    2.   The decisions of the closing of the Armenian atomic energy plant and of the Nayirit factories;[20]

    3.   The resolution condemning the 1915 Genocide of the Armenian people;[21]

---

[17] While it is difficult to categorize clearly, one can count up to six political organizations with enough following to have elected members to the Parliament in which the Communist Party won 25% of the seats and the Armenian National Movement 40%. The ANM-led coalition of democratic forces has the support of about 70% of the Parliament.

[18] The beginning of perestroika is associated with the election of Mikhail Gorbachev to the post of First Secretary of the USSR Communist Party in March 1985.

[19] A similar situation occurred in 1905, during the First Russian Revolution, in many parts of the Russian Empire, including Eastern Armenia.

[20] See note 15.

[21] While there had been many symbolic acts of recognition of the Genocide

4. The decisions to recognize May 28 as the date of the reestablishment of Armenian statehood and the tricolor as a national symbol;[22]

5. The formal recognition of a number of political organizations;

6. The adoption of Article 75 as part of the Armenian constitution guaranteeing the supremacy of Armenian laws;

7. The temporary stop to the 1990 spring military draft;[23]

8. The decree of the education ministry regarding the obligatory Armenian education of Armenian children, etc.[24]

It may not be superfluous to remember that it was as a result of the tremendous efforts by that popular movement that many freedoms now enjoyed were established in the republic, including freedom of speech, press, demonstrations, and meetings, as well as the relatively democratic electoral laws [that produced] the multiplicity of opinions in this Parliament.[25]

---

against Armenians under Ottoman rule in Western Armenia, this was the first such resolution by the Supreme Soviet of Armenia.

Because of Turkey's active campaign against the recognition of the Genocide, Moscow has always tried to minimize the damage such a recognition can do to its diplomatic and political ties to Turkey. At the same time, Moscow had tolerated semi-formal recognition of the Genoçide by Soviet authorities in Armenia as one way of keeping a sense of physical danger alive.

[22] May 28, 1918 is the date when the Republic of Armenia was founded following the withdrawal of the Russian army from the Caucasus front, and the defeat by a makeshift Armenian army of the much weakened Turkish army. Soviet historiography has always recognized November 29, 1920—the official date of the overthrow of the "bourgeois" republic through a socialist "revolution" from within—as the birth date of modern Armenia. The Hunchakian and Ramgavar parties in the diaspora have followed official Soviet dogma. Only the Dashnaktsutiune has continued to celebrate May 28 as the date of Armenia's independence. See also Document One, notes 19, 51, 63, 67, and 68.

The "tricolor" (red, blue, and orange, horizontal) was the flag of the independent republic. The last flag of Soviet Armenia was red, blue, and red. For decades, the tricolor was banned in Armenia. In the diaspora, it had become the symbol of conflict and divisions.

[23] Draft calls in the USSR are sent twice a year, in the spring and the fall.

[24] One of the major propellents of the movement, including its drive toward independence, has been the fear of Russification. For those concerned with this phenomenon the most dangerous sign is the increasing number of Armenian students who attended "Russian" schools, or schools with Russian "orientation."

[25] The most important change in the electoral laws concerned the elimination of the rule assigning a number of seats to institutions and organizations. Given Communist Party control of public life, these seats were certain to go to Party members. The new Parliament also assigned 12 seats to representatives from Mountainous Karabagh.

These successes, too, are the obvious guarantees of the democratic forces [substantiating] their claim for the vote of confidence of this parliament and of the people during the current struggle for power.

Thus, if there is today a power in the republic which has the ability to take the republic out of its perilous state and make a sharp turn toward the achievement of its national goals, it is the democratic wing of Armenia's Supreme Soviet. This wing is democratic not only by its ideology but also by its organization. Its movement involves representatives of all classes—workers, engineers, doctors, teachers, junior researchers, intellectuals, etc., while the representatives of the so-called [Communist] Party of the workers and peasants in this Supreme Soviet are exclusively from the nomenklatura.[26] Food for thought for our people.

The experience too of Eastern Europe, the Baltic republics, and finally Russia must suggest which are the political forces the people trust to realize their goals and how important it is to make the right choice at the right time. In that respect, the example of the Ukraine is most enlightening. Only a few months after it was formed, the Ukrainian parliament had to free itself of the control of the party bureaucracy and, with some delay, adopt the path of the establishment of national sovereignty.[27] The same may threaten Armenia if we make the wrong choice now. However, while the Ukraine may afford the luxury of a delay, we cannot, given the seriousness of the situation in the republic and in Artsakh.

Today we are facing a number of immediate problems. In addition to the long term programs, [we must deal with] the problem of Artsakh, the reconstruction of the disaster area, the improvement of the condition of the refugees,[28] the restitution of an economy in ruins, etc.

But neither these problems nor the long term projects can be realized until the new government can stabilize the situation

---

[26] Term to indicate the privileged elements of the Communist Party who had access to positions, Western goods, and perks.

[27] Reference to the first elections in the Ukraine where most former officials were reelected and charged with the implementation of a new program. The experiment did not work.

[28] Refers to close to 200,000 Armenians of Azerbaijan who, since February 1988 have flocked into Armenia. The bulk of these refugees came when an informal exchange of populations between the two republics was arranged in November 1989, at which time approximately 150,000 Azeri Turks moved from Armenia to Azerbaijan. The balance has come during and after the intermittent pogroms against Armenians during the past two years in various cities of Azerbaijan, including Sumgait, Kirovapat, and Baku. See also Document Four, note 54.

within the republic. Without that stability, it is impossible to realize any economic, political, or national program; it is impossible to sign international agreements, it is impossible to introduce foreign capital.

The [current government] cannot bring that stability because it does not enjoy the confidence of the people.

Document Seven

Declaration on Armenia's Independence by the Parliament of Armenia

This document constitutes the first major statement of the new, democratically elected Parliament of Armenia. The goal of independence is legitimized by the need of the nation to resolve its problems in a democratic and sovereign state, by international law and practice, and by the precedent of independence from 1918-1920.

It should be noted that the document is a declaration on, rather than of, independence. It sets no deadlines. It allows the republic to make preparations for independence where and when feasible. It reflects the determination as well as the flexibility of the new government. Above all, the Declaration on Independence sets the framework for intellectual and political development, standards by which society's evolution must be measured.

Armenia accepted the document with a mixture of contentment and pensiveness. Upon reading this text, Mikhail Gorbachev is reported to have said, "These Armenians seem to be smarter than I thought. You could never tell from this document whether they are in the Union or out." The document found little echo in the Western press,[1] and less so in Western diplomatic statements. The Armenian diaspora accepted it with some bewilderment. [2]

---

[1] *The New York Times* mentioned it in one sentence in an unrelated story. See Document Four, note 29.

[2] Some of the most commonly asked questions were: "Can they do that?" "What will Moscow say?" "Will Turkey let us be?" "Can we govern ourselves?" "How will we feed our people?" With some exceptions, the diaspora Armenian press reported the event largely as a matter of fact, rarely with much enthusiasm, until a few days had passed and Armenia was still there. One of the more significant positions was taken by the Dashnaktsutiune. During a tour of US cities coinciding with the adoption of the declaration, Nazaret Berberian, editor of the Dashnaktsutiune Bureau organ *Droshak*, claimed that the right to choose the moment for the declaration of Armenia's independence belongs to the

The Supreme Soviet of the Armenian SSR

Expressing the united will of the Armenian people;

Aware of its historic responsibility for the destiny of the Armenian people and engaged in the realization of the aspirations of all Armenians and the restoration of historical justice;

Proceeding from the principles of the Universal Declaration on Human Rights and the generally recognized norms of international law;

Exercising the right of nations to free self-determination;

Based on the December 1, 1989, joint decision of the Armenian SSR Supreme Soviet and the Artsakh National Council on the "Reunification of the Armenian SSR and Mountainous Region of Karabagh;"

[Intent on] developing the democratic traditions of the independent Republic of Armenia established on May 28, 1918;

Positing the problem of the creation of a democratic society and a society based on the rule of law,

Declares

The beginning of the process of establishing independent statehood.

1. The Armenian SSR is renamed the Republic of Armenia (Armenia). The Republic of Armenia shall have its flag, coat of arms, and anthem.[3]

2. The Republic of Armenia is a self-governing state, endowed with the supremacy of state authority, independence, sovereignty, and plenipotentiary power.

Only the Constitution and laws of the Republic of Armenia are valid for the whole territory of the Republic of Armenia.

3. The bearer of Armenian statehood is the people of the Republic of Armenia, which executes its authority directly and through its representative bodies on the basis of the Constitution and laws of the Republic of Armenia. The right to speak on behalf of the people of the Republic belongs exclusively to the Supreme Soviet of Armenia.

4. All citizens living on the territory of Armenia are granted

---

Dashnaktsutiune. Subsequently, the *Droshak* claimed that the Declaration was inspired largely by the Dashnaktsutiune position. To reach that point, claimed the *Droshak,* the new government had had to discard many of the misconceptions and erroneous notions it held as leadership of the ANM, before coming to power.

[3] Subsequently the tricolor of the independent republic (red, blue, orange) was reinstated as the flag of the republic. See also Document Six, note 22.

The new anthem and coat of arms will be determined through an international competition.

citizenship of the Republic of Armenia. Armenians of the diaspora have the right of citizenship of Armenia.

The citizens of the Republic of Armenia are protected and aided by the republic.

The Republic of Armenia guarantees the free and equal development of its citizens, regardless of national origin, race, or creed.

5. With the purpose of guaranteeing the security of the Republic of Armenia and the inviolability of its borders, the Republic of Armenia creates its own armed forces, internal troops, organs of state, and public security under the jurisdiction of the Supreme Soviet.

The Republic of Armenia has its share of the USSR military apparatus.

The Republic of Armenia determines the regulation of military service for its citizens independently.

Military units of other countries, their military bases and building complexes can be located on the territory of the Republic of Armenia only by a decision of Armenia's Supreme Soviet.

The armed forces of the Republic of Armenia can be deployed only by a decision of its Supreme Soviet.

6. As a sovereign state under international law, the Republic of Armenia conducts an independent foreign policy; it establishes direct relations with other states, national state units of the USSR, and participates in the activity of international organizations.

7. The national wealth of the Republic of Armenia—the land, the earth's crust, airspace, water and other natural resources, [as well as] the economic, intellectual, cultural capabilities are the property of its people. The regulation of their governance, usage and possession is determined by the laws of the Republic of Armenia.

The Republic of Armenia has the right to its share of the USSR national wealth, including the supplies of gold and diamond, and hard currency funds.

8. The Republic of Armenia determines the principles and regulation of its economic system, creates its own money, national bank, finance-loan system, tax and customs services, based on the system of multiple forms of property ownership.

9. On its territory the Republic of Armenia guarantees freedom of speech, press, and conscience; separation of legislative, executive, and judicial powers; a multi-party system; equality of political parties under the law; depoliticization of law enforcement bodies and armed forces.

10. The Republic of Armenia guarantees the use of Armenian

as the state language in all spheres of the republic's life; the Republic creates its own system of education and of scientific and cultural development.

11. The Republic of Armenia stands in support of the task of [achieving] international recognition of the 1915 Genocide in Ottoman Turkey and Western Armenia.[4]

12. This declaration serves as a basis for the development of the constitution for the Republic of Armenia and, until such time [as the new constitution is approved], as the basis for the introduction of amendments to the current constitution; [and] for the operation of state authorities and the development of new legislation for the Republic.

Declaration first adopted on August 23, 1990 by a vote of 183-2-2, and with minor amendments on August 25, 1990]

Signed by

Levon Ter Petrosian
President of the Supreme Soviet
of the Republic of Armenia

Ara Sahakian
Secretary of the Supreme Soviet
of the Republic of Armenia
Yerevan

---

[4] This was one of the more controversial and emotional issues debated. One side argued that historical events had no place in a document to be used as the basis of the Constitution and that reference in the preamble to historical justice was adequate to cover the matter of the Genocide. Others, including organizations from the diaspora, pleaded for the inclusion of an article on claims arising from the Genocide.

This formulation does not seem to have satisfied the second group. The Ramgavar Party, for example, which has generally supported the new government, has complained that the article does not discuss territorial claims arising from the Genocide.

Document Eight

LEVON TER PETROSIAN

The State of the Republic

President Levon Ter Petrosian took the podium of the Parliament on October 22, 1990 to give his assessment of the situation in Armenia, focusing mainly on its relations with Moscow. This "State of the Republic" address continues to reflect the basic belief by the new leaders of Armenia that the USSR is in a process of disintegration and the vital interest of Armenia requires that the process evolve in an orderly manner, without the use of force from above and without artificial enhancements from below.

The speech was reproduced in the October 23, 1990 issue of Hayastani Hanrapetutiun *(Republic of Armenia), the Parliament's own new publication.*

The fall of the Roman Empire convinced mankind that there was no eternity. It is also clear that the last of the colonial systems, i.e. the Soviet empire, had to reach the brink of collapse.

Perhaps this was a revelation for our people which has been in a slumber. But events of the last few years were pointing in that direction. Driven by objective factors, that collapse is becoming a reality.

And today there is one thing left for us—for all the peoples of the Soviet Union—and the world community to do: Help make that collapse as painless, as bloodless as possible; make the transition to a new system peaceful. The experience of the Eastern European countries can inspire the confidence in us that this is possible, that the leaders of the Soviet Union and its republics display enough tolerance and consciousness to avoid major confrontations and upheavals.

But the Soviet Union, just as other collapsing, faltering empires is exerting its last efforts to preserve its territorial integrity and the totalitarian structure. For those purposes, the empire has and uses very effective levers: Political, economic, ethnic/national, and military.

It is possible to assert that the political lever has exhausted itself with the declarations of sovereignty and independence. The command from the center has dissipated in those republics which have embarked upon the road to democracy. A majority of the republics have asserted the supremacy of their constitutions and laws. This change is already a functioning mechanism because the central bodies have lost their political authority, because, as a rule, their decisions are not implemented in the republics. We must add to this march toward disintegration the bankruptcy of the ideology which was the foundation of the communist political regime. Consequently, the center must now seek other levers.

The most effective alternative lever is, of course, the economic one. With the loss of political control, it is very likely that the central authorities will resort to economic pressures to keep the republics in line.[1]

The central authorities control the systems of distribution, banking, money supply, foreign commerce, and foreign currency. It appears that the central authorities will use all of these activities to preserve the totalitarian system. In the economic sector, there are additional factors that may reduce the pace of the movement toward disintegration. While many republics have made clear their intention to become independent, it seems that they are still trying to preserve the economic relations developed within the Union, fearful of the uncertainties of the future. The republics are trying, nonetheless, to replace vertical relations with horizontal ones, i.e. within the context of agreements signed between the republics.[2]

However effective the economic lever may be, conceptually the direction of the central authorities is in deep conflict with the processes and fundamental concept of economic development of the country. The latter are defined by the principle of decentralization, which can only strengthen the economic sovereignty of republics. Moscow's use of the economic lever will produce a negative reaction and will not contribute to the preservation of the territorial integrity of the country. This conflict is an objec-

---

[1] At different times and in different forms the Kremlin has used this lever against Armenia, Georgia, Lithuania, Latvia, and Estonia. By refusing to pay the full amount designated as its portion of the federal budget, the Russian Federation reversed the threat in January 1991.

[2] Armenia has signed such agreements with a number of republics. An agreement with Russia is drafted and awaits finalization.

tive reality; if the country really wants to resolve the economic crisis, it has no other course [but decentralization]. The economic lever disrupts the objective process of development and for that reason it too is condemned to failure.[3]

The next lever which the central authorities may use to preserve the status quo is the increase and exploitation of tensions between nationalities. The Soviet Union, like other colonial empires, has used, is using, and will use this lever, from which we have suffered most.[4]

Despite the painful events that have already occurred in this respect, we must hope that Soviet peoples will find enough strength within themselves to distinguish their interests from those of the empire.

Finally, one must not rule out the use of brute force, the fourth lever. For all practical purposes, the central authorities have only this authority. Only the army, the forces of the interior ministry and the KGB submit to the central authorities. It is possible that the availability of these forces may lead the central authorities to their use. We have already seen the use of this lever in some cases, even though in some cases justifiably— such as in Azerbaijan where there was an attempt to overthrow the legitimate government by force and the government reacted similarly by the use of force.[5] Nonetheless there are now developments in some regions of the country where the use of force may lead to a general conflagration. It is also noticeable that the central authorities are displaying much tolerance toward illegal and violent actions which once would have invited immediate reaction. This indicates that the central authorities are cognizant of the huge responsibilities they have. The use of force is tantamount to resigning from a policy of development. This too must give us some confidence, since the center has thus far been circumspect and it has used force only in extreme circumstances.[6]

---

[3] At the end Gorbachev may be unwilling to pay the political price for economic development.

[4] Reference to the use of pogroms in Azerbaijan to derail reform movements and increase tensions between Armenians and Azerbaijanis which, in turn, makes central authority indispensable as peacemaker. See also Document Four, notes 38 and 45.

[5] The Soviet army overran Baku in January 1990, ostensibly to save the Armenians of the city from pogroms. The army in fact intervened only when the mob attacked Communist Party headquarters, five days after the start of the pogroms.

[6] Kremlin reintroduced the use of force, this time against Lithuania, on January 13, 1991. Levon Ter Petrosian was asked to head a delegation empow-

In addition to the processes in the Soviet Union, developments in the Transcaucasus too are of essential importance for our republic. What has transpired in the Transcaucasus? In Armenia, we have witnessed the establishment of a democratic regime; Communist rule has ended. Azerbaijan has gone in the opposite direction: Communist rule has become more entrenched. Georgia is in an unstable, pre-electoral state. It is difficult to predict what will be the result of elections.[7]

It may seem that the situation in the region now roughly parallels that of 1920. Communist Azerbaijan has become the base from which central authorities can do battle against Armenia and, if need be, Georgia. And we see the cooperation of Azerbaijan and central authorities in Artsakh. This cooperation may give Azerbaijan temporary benefits and, apparently, it is doing so.

But, as pointed out above, this is just the appearance, since the situation is fundamentally different. If in 1920 Azerbaijan came forth as the ally of a Bolshevik Russia that was getting stronger, Azerbaijan today is the base of support for a Soviet center that has lost its real authority. Azerbaijan then is in opposition not only to Armenia but also to democratic Russia. This difference signals a change in our perception of the current situation; it also provides us with wide opportunities for maneuvering. We must appreciate this subtle difference and benefit from it. I have in mind the possibility of serious economic and political relations with Russia based on the common interests of our two republics. One indication of such a possibility is my meeting with Boris Yeltsin and the correspondence that followed it, the echo of that correspondence in the Russian parliament, and a very important and favorable decision taken by the parliament.[8]

The political consciousness of the Armenian people has undergone essential changes under the light of recent events in the

---

ered by the Federation Council (presidents of republics and regions) to mediate between the USSR and Lithuania.

[7] Georgia elected a nationalist government headed by Zviad Gamsakhurdia.

[8] Probably a reference to the position propounded by Boris Yeltsin and adopted by the Parliament of the Russian Federation that Russian draftees in the USSR armed forces should not be sent to quell domestic, ethnic conflicts. This is seen as a major step toward the stabilization of the situation on Mountainous Karabagh where the presence of Soviet forces on the side of Azerbaijanis is allowing the Azerbaijani side to sustain an intransigent position. The Azerbaijani belief that they can force their rule upon Karabagh with the help of the army, even if it means forcing Armenians to leave, is the basis of their refusal to enter meaningful negotiations.

Soviet Union and the Transcaucasus. The Armenian people finally woke up from its delightful slumber to suddenly discover that the Soviet Union cannot provide eternal safeguards for its existence. Witness the massacres of Sumgait, Kirovapat, and Baku;[9] the hundreds of thousands of refugees; the economic blockades of Artsakh and Armenia; and the prospect of Soviet armies leaving the Transcaucasus.[10]

Faced with the shock of this realization, and the bitter experience, the Armenian political mind and the developing liberation movement reached the conclusion that the Armenian nation must create, through its own strength, new guarantees for its existence; these guarantees must be real, not imaginary.

The first guarantee is the replacement of the communist government—a government which was directed from the outside and served foreign interests—with a democratic government that conducts a national policy. We must rule out the management of national affairs by alien forces and make possible the development of policies that serve solely the interests of our own people.

This change has already occurred, but only partially, only in the upper echelons of the government.

The final step in that direction is tied to the forthcoming local elections.[11]

A second guarantee will have been secured when, in matters of [social and economic] development, we move ahead of our neighbors Georgia and Azerbaijan with whom we can compete neither in human nor in natural resources.[12] Our only advantage with regard to them will be our being far ahead in devel-

[9] Cities in Azerbaijan where a series of anti-Armenian pogroms, between February 1988 and January 1990, caused the death of hundreds and the deportation of more than 300,000 Armenians.

[10] The Russian army on the Turkish front disintegrated in early 1918, following the Bolshevik Revolution, forcing Armenians to face the Turkish army alone. This "defenselessness" has left a deep scar on Armenian collective memory.

[11] The deeply entrenched power structure nourished by the Communist Party has been in a position to block the policies of the new government. Local elections in November 1990 were inconclusive, partially because of the power of intimidation which local officials (associated with the former regime) had over voters, as well as due to voter apathy. To break the cycle, in early December 1990, Prime Minister Vazgen Manukian requested and received from Parliament extraordinary powers that included the right to appoint local officials.

[12] The work force in Armenia is highly educated and skilled. The comment must be a reference to the numbers.

opment. We have already fulfilled, in the republic, a major precondition in this respect—the establishment of a democratic regime.

Assisted by the freedoms enjoyed under democracy and the possibilities offered by a sovereign national policy, Armenia can move ahead of its two neighbors by implementing radical reforms that ensure its social and economic development. Legislation regarding private property and land reform are of major significance for such reforms. Legislation in these two areas will enable the Armenian people to externalize its natural aptitude in business and sense of initiative—both wrested criminally from its hands during the last 70 years. It was due to these aptitudes that Armenians had earned dominant positions in the economic lives of Tbilisi and Baku.[13] It is due to these aptitudes that our diasporan brethren have acquired prominent positions in the business world under conditions of harsh competition.

It is not incidental that the first pieces of legislation to be presented by our government to the Parliament will deal with property and land.

Another important factor in our ability to develop ahead of our neighbors is the existence of the diaspora, whose material, political, and intellectual capabilities can be of essential help to the welfare of our republic.

The third guarantee for the existence and security of the Armenian state will be the creation of our own armed forces. A state cannot exist without an army. The experience of 1918 and 1942 shows that at the most critical moments our nation's military force was outside the boundaries of the republic. That is the reason why the Armenian National Movement included the creation of our own armed forces in its first program.

There are today a number of proposals on how to create that force. Many are of the naive opinion that such a force can be created based on the militia. It is clear, however, that the country will be defended by a professional army. There is a more natural, a more reasonable path, available to the other republics of the Union too: The representative of each nation must serve on the territory of his republic.

---

[13] Before the 1917 Revolution, Armenians constituted an important minority in Baku and a majority of the population of Tbilisi. Armenians played a significant, if not dominant, role in finance, manufacturing, and the professions in both capitals. Large numbers were also simple laborers or factory workers. Over 250,000 Armenians continue to live in Tbilisi, while the 200,000 or so in Baku were uprooted in January 1990.

At the present time there are 40,000 Armenian soldiers serving [in the Soviet army] outside Armenia. Even if they continue to serve the Soviet army on Armenian territory, it is clear that [when stationed in Armenia] they could fulfill their duty toward the fatherland in case of danger.

This is the path we should choose. It is possible to say that the Parliament of Armenia has taken very realistic steps by stopping the spring and fall drafts. Sooner or later the commanders of the Soviet army will have to come to terms with this fact and create the conditions necessary for these young men to do their service in Armenia. Our projections must take into account the possibility that the Soviet army may some day leave Armenia. At the same time we should not forget that Russia has strategic interests that have evolved over the centuries and, that it cannot abandon them overnight.

At any rate, we must probably reconcile for a while with the idea of continued Russian army bases in Armenia.

The fourth guarantee consists of a breakthrough in the political isolation of Armenia and the development of our own foreign policy which we have been denied during the past 70 years. During that time we did not even have direct relations with other Soviet republics. We must now develop that policy. We must also seek membership in international organizations. It appears that very soon we may have our own representatives, even if in an informal capacity, in the United States and France. It is necessary to expand to any degree possible our relations with all international organizations. There are such possibilities and we have already taken the first steps.

And, finally, the most important and fifth guarantee which is mandatory for the normal development of any country. That is the establishment of orderly relations with our immediate neighbors. The basis of these relations will be the pragmatism derived from our national interests. This point has been the subject of controversy and has been exploited for political purposes. But healthy elements have understood the imperative of this safeguard. And it is the authorities of Armenia that must develop and conduct this policy. I am sure that the Armenian people, who have reached a high level of political maturity, are now in a position to separate their national interests from the exploitation of ideas for political purposes.

The agenda of the Armenian people is to give our republic economic and political sovereignty, an organism that functions on its own, that derives maximum benefit from favorable internal and international circumstances and is able to face, in time, predictable political and economic dangers.

It is time, finally, that we study seriously the lessons of our bitter historical experience; instead of an audacious, romantic nation, we must become a cold, realistic and pragmatic nation, whose each step must be circumspect, based on concrete and faultless calculation.

The ability to maneuver and a flexible diplomacy must become the main weapons of our policy. We must follow closely the relations of our friends and antagonists and derive some benefit from even the slightest of the conflicts between them. For that reason it is necessary to forgo, once and for all, *demonstrative*, frivolous actions. On the one hand such actions provoke our friends and antagonists; on the other hand, failing to produce positive results, they produce deep disaffection among the masses.

Politics is a system, not the simple addition of incidental acts. Therefore, no elected government that has a developed policy, has the right to pay tribute to tangential pressures or to digress from the fundamental direction it has adopted because of such pressures.[14] A complex of policies can be countered by another complex of policies and not by demands for isolated actions that merely oppose them. This does not mean, of course, that the system is a dogma and cannot be corrected as the need arises.

To summarize this analysis, the policies adopted by the democratic government of Armenia can be stated in the following words: To create new and stable political safeguards for the existence and development of our republic calmly, with subtle maneuvers, through supple diplomacy, slowly but steadily, avoiding grave confrontations, and without superfluous demonstrations and haste. By realizing these goals we will have fulfilled our responsibilities toward the next generations, leaving them the task of realizing our other national dreams.

Reality is not frozen history; however stable, it is subject to unexpected upheavals. By creating the safeguards for the existence of our nation we will be ready to benefit from those upheavals.

Time has given us real opportunities to set the foundations for the actualization of our national aspirations. Not to benefit from these opportunities would be unforgivable mindlessness.

---

[14] The comment is a reference to the attitude adopted by some groups opposing the government's position on isolated issues, thus endearing themselves to single issue constituencies or reducing a political program into a single issue.

Document Nine

LEVON TER PETROSIAN

The State of the Union

> President Levon Ter Petrosian delivered this address in November 1990 to the Supreme Soviet of the USSR. Together with his speech to the Armenian Parliament the month before (Document Eight), they cover the full range of foreign and domestic issues facing Armenia and the way Armenia's current leadership seeks to resolve them.
>
> Ter Petrosian brings to the understanding of the state of the Soviet Union the same simple and compelling logic which he and other movement leaders have displayed since early 1988 in their analysis of Armenia's strengths, weaknesses, and real possibilities.
>
> The text of this speech was published in the November 16, 1990 issue of Hayastani Hanrapetutiun.

Honorable Members,

The current debate in this chamber is, of course, interesting. But it is no more than that. If it continues in this vein and we leave this chamber without having adopted concrete mechanisms to resolve the current situation, I am confident we will have to return within a week or two and examine a situation even more critical. Unfortunately I did not see such mechanisms being proposed either by the President[1] or by the other speakers. I agree with the factual observations made in all of the speeches, although it seems the emphasis is being placed on negative aspects of our situation. You are all aware that along with the negative, our reality has also some positive dimensions. Allow me to name a few.

The first is that the process of attaining sovereignty by the republics is deepening and the prerogatives of the central authorities and the republics are being delineated.

---

[1] Mikhail S. Gorbachev.

The second is the establishment of horizontal relations between the republics.

The third is the strengthening of the processes of democratization within the republics, something no one can deny.

The fourth, and the most important, is the increasing vitality and strengthening of the republics. Some republics, at any rate, have demonstrated such a trend by deeds.

Now, briefly, concerning negative aspects.

It is obvious, there is chaos in the economy, social and interethnic relations are strained, authorities have been paralyzed [as if] by a stroke, etc. I believe we are now facing a completely new situation, one that has warranted this gathering. This is now the new critical state of the government. The stroke has now brought [the patient] to the throes of death, because, in my view, in addition to all the above, there is hanging over our heads the threat of a "right wing" danger. There is such a threat, as well as a threat of social "bund." Naturally, we must not lose our heads. It is our duty, our responsibility, to carefully seek a way out of this situation.

I propose a series of approaches. The President proposed a freezing of decisions by the governments of republics. I think it is very clear that this will not pass. Others—not only in this hall but also the public opinion and media—are suggesting that the government be given more powers. Some here expressed similar notions. Unfortunately, many see only one meaning in the term "government," i.e. a repressive body. But we are forgetting its main meaning, the government as an agency that regulates.

What are the mechanisms of regulation? Consultations, the traditional consultations, are no longer fruitful. The use of force, I have already stated, is not desirable and is dangerous. Coordination? This institution, too, no longer exists. Appeals to reason belong to a distant past. Presidential decrees? These too have no effect. The only mechanism which has demonstrated its vitality—each of you can testify to that—is the [governing by] *agreement*.[2] A preservation instinct, a sense of danger become activated at critical times. At that moment [government by] agreement is really possible. Such agreements, I am sure, we have all achieved between political parties, between organizations. Such mechanisms are now functioning in the Russian Federation and in the Baltic region. The three Baltic republics have been functioning on that principle for some time now. Agreement is the only mechanism which is functioning today.

---

[2] The term *agreement* has connotations of consent, consensus, and coordination.

But which is the governmental body that is equipped to put into place such a mechanism? The parliament of the Union [Peoples' Congress]? I think it is clear to all of us that that body is an anachronism. The Supreme Soviet is adopting resolutions, wonderful decisions, which remain in the books. But there is no reason to despair. I do not think your work is in vain. At any rate, this body has great inherent strength. I am saying this without irony. Your labors here are not in vain. Your decisions, your resolutions are helping the republics develop their own laws. It is possible to be satisfied with as much.

What other bodies are there? The Council of Ministers is suffering from an obsession to assume too much power and under the new circumstances is incapable of ruling by agreement. The President? I already stated my view on that option. I believe the presidential institution too is not as yet ready to assume such a role. This means we must seek, we must create new organs that are capable of functioning on the principle of agreement. What are these organs?

The only thing we can do now, the only mechanism we can use at this moment, even on a temporary—say a one year—basis is to create a Committee for Economic Agreement. This Committee can be constituted as the presidium of the Council of Ministers and may be made up of the Presidents of the Councils of Ministers of the 15 republics. The President of the USSR Council of Ministers then implements the decisions of those 15 officials. It is possible to prepare here the status and by-laws of that presidium.

The second organ could be the Committee for Political Agreement. Such a body does exist formally; it is the Council of the USSR Federation. But in my view that body still does not have its statutes.[3] Moreover, as a member of that body I do not know what my prerogatives are. The Supreme Soviet of Armenia has not given me the authority to endorse or reject any resolution or sign any document. Here too it is necessary to decide on statutes and by-laws. It is necessary to determine, for example, the kind of majority needed to adopt policies.

---

[3] On January 13, 1991, following the Soviet army's violent intervention in Vilnius, the Federation Council dispatched a delegation to Lithuania on a fact finding mission and a search for a political solution. Levon Ter Petrosian was asked to head the delegation because, wrote *New York Times* reporter Bill Keller, he "has emphasized careful political negotiation and conciliation to resolve some explosive difficulties in Armenia." Other observers were quick to point out that should this mission succeed, the Federation Council may, in fact, become a source of authority.

Finally, some comments on the Union treaty. In my view we have already missed the moment when it was possible to sign such a treaty. It is impossible to achieve that now, half way in the process. The republics are undergoing deepening processes leading them to sovereignty, toward the delineation of their rights vis à vis the central government, and it is not possible to sign that treaty at this point. It is necessary to allow these processes to reach their logical conclusion and only then sign a new treaty. A Union treaty should have been signed either when the republics were just beginning to look at their sovereignty issues or it should be signed when these processes are completed.

If such mechanisms are created and justify themselves, it then becomes possible to use this experience to determine the real shape of the future Union.

I offer my apologies if I sounded didactic at all and thank you for your attention.

Appendices

Appendix A

Democracy and Diaspora Politics

Appendix A-One

Joint Statement by the Three Armenian Political Parties In the Diaspora

A joint statement by the three diasporan parties[1] is a rare occurrence in recent memory. Except on major anniversaries of the Genocide, parties have found little reason to work together.[2] This document is all the more remarkable for the basis of unity which the three parties found: Changes in Armenia should not be introduced at the expense of the regime.[3]

With this Statement, the signatories placed themselves on the side of a government that had shown little reason to develop or support a national agenda, however defined. This was understandable, given its source of legitimacy and power.[4]

The next Document (Appendix A2) was one of the responses, probably the most noteworthy, which different groups and individuals in Armenia and the diaspora made to the Joint Statement.

[1] See Document One, notes 63, 67, and 68.

[2] Their disagreements have been strongest, and their confrontations fiercest, on the question of the legitimacy of the Soviet annexation of Armenia and of the Communist regime there.

The Ramgavar and Hunchakian parties have been supporting the regime for decades while the Dashnaktsutiune had been opposing it, until recently. Until recently, too, the Dashnaktsutiune had been advocating independence as a viable goal, while the first two had been ridiculing it.

[3] The Joint Statement is representative of the position of parties in the diaspora regarding the movement. The Ramgavar Party English language organ *The Armenian Mirror-Spectator,* published in Massachusetts, for example, failed to mention the "Karabagh Committee" throughout 1988 until the members of the Committee were imprisoned and the international human rights community took note of them as political prisoners. In response to criticisms from members, the Dashnaktsutiune leadership argued that the Joint Statement had been misunderstood and may have been badly edited. Yet a statement it released in the name of representatives of its own National Committees meeting in Paris in late 1988 included the following: "Outbursts of protest must not become open forums for irresponsible elements; and, especially, these must not serve to discredit or damage the leadership of Armenia, which is finally demonstrating an effort to support and protect the Artsakh Movement" (*Droshak*, May 1989, p.5).

[4] At least politically this orientation proved to be a miscalculation for the signatories, however, as the government was voted out of office on the first opportunity the voters had.

The original text of the Joint Statement was written in Armenian and published in the press in October 1988. An English translation, which should be considered official, appeared in the May 1989 issue of Droshak, *the official organ of the Dashnaktsutiune. The following is an edited version of that translation where glaring errors have been hopefully avoided.*

The crisis of Armenians in the Autonomous Region of Mountainous Karabagh has acquired serious dimensions and has become the crisis of Armenians everywhere—in Mother Armenia as well as in the diaspora.

From the outset, the three Armenian national political organizations, which have followed events in Karabagh, have been concerned with this crisis. [The parties] have expressed, through a united front and on several occasions, their full and unreserved solidarity with the people of Karabagh and Armenia and their support of their just cause. The parties consider the reunification of Mountainous Karabagh with Soviet Armenia the final resolution of that cause.

Today, with this joint statement, we come once more to express our unfaltering support to our people in Karabagh and Armenia and their respective state authorities with the hope of a just solution to their united, unremitting, and determined stance.[5]

Our expectation and demand from the higher responsible bodies of the Soviet Union is that, as positive evidence of a fair-minded approach, all those individuals and groups responsible for the crimes committed against Armenians in Sumgait[6] and Karabagh be publicly tried and duly sentenced.

---

[5] By also supporting the authorities, the document ignores the social and political dimensions of the mass movement. Long after the movement had become a drive toward democracy and raised substantial questions on the legitimacy and credibility of the government, diasporan parties were determining that the masses were wrong and the discredited Communist Party could regain legitimacy if it only adopted a pro-Karabagh position.

[6] This document is significant in many respects. Other than supporting the reunification of Karabagh to Armenia, the signatories seem to be most comfortable when dealing with the demand that those guilty for the Sumgait pogroms be punished, a sensitive issue considering the place of Genocide and of the non-recognition of the Genocide in Armenian, especially in diasporan, consciousness.

The document ignores the political dimension of Sumgait. Rather than an expression of "Turkish" behavior, Sumgait may have been an attempt, inspired by higher authorities, to change the agenda from reform, democratization, and destalinization to law and order.

We also expect that the Soviet news media in Moscow, as well as in Armenia, will have a thorough and accurate coverage of events and criminal acts in the region from the viewpoint of both reportage and analysis, and pursuant to the acclaimed spirit and laudable principles of the policy of glasnost announced by the higher Soviet authorities.

We demand that the leadership of Soviet Armenia, adding to its resolve to become the legitimate interpreter of the rightful claims of the Armenian masses, adopts the Karabagh issue as its priority agendum, striving to bring it to a just and comprehensible solution. At the same time, the republic's leadership should deem unacceptable and incongruous with the claims of the people of Armenia all those initiatives brought to bear up to this point.

We also call upon our valiant brethren in Armenia and Karabagh to forgo such extreme acts as work stoppages, student strikes, and some radical calls and expressions that unsettle law and order in public life in the homeland; that subject to heavy losses the economic, productive, educational, and cultural life; that [harm seriously] the good standing of our nation in its relations with the higher Soviet bodies and other Soviet republics.[7] These zealous attitudes also provide for the ulterior motives of the enemies of our people.

Above all, we should safeguard the unity of our people, wherein lies our strength, and we should pursue our ultimate interests with farsightedness and determination.

Central Executive of the Hunchakian Social Democratic Party
Bureau of the Armenian Revolutionary Federation-
  Dashnaktsutiune
Central Executive of the Ramgavar Liberal Party

---

[7] Calls for "law and order" in a non-democratic society amount to denying people the tools of resistance and pressure. The impact of appeals to end demonstrations and strikes, lest economic life be disrupted in a bankrupt economy supported by a hated regime, is to give aid and comfort to the regime. The signatories may have been motivated by the fear of not being liked by "higher" authorities or by a naive belief in the economy as a sphere independent of and unrelated to politics. Both reasons are common to diasporan and colonial mentalities. Regardless, the Joint Statement displayed a marked absence of understanding of the role of people in politics and of popular movements in history.

Appendix A-Two

The Fatherland and the Diaspora

> I love the sunset in the autumn, when
> The red sun burns everything
>
> *Hagopjan Tadevosian*

The previous document was a milestone in diaspora political thinking and in Armenia-Diaspora relations, as it crystalized the position of diaspora political organizations. More importantly, it marked the beginning of an important process in Armenia. Public organizations, movement leaders, and common people began to disabuse themselves of certain myths regarding diasporan organizations. Until then the diaspora was assigned a much larger role in the realization of the national agenda or agendas conceived in Armenia by the various organizations making up the movement. This document indicates that the assignments had to be reviewed and adjusted. It is the most poignant and perceptive of the formal responses. It also comes from an organization, the National Self-Determination Group led by Paruyr Hayrikian, whose vision of a strategy for independence had relied most heavily on strong diasporan support and cooperation. This support was expected particularly from the Dashnaktsutiune which was known for its championing the cause of independence for Armenia and which had been constantly abused in Soviet propaganda.

This response was written for the editorial board of and published in Hayrenik (Yerevan), *the organ of the National Self- Determination Group.*

Your silence was insulting; but your words were even more so.

We learned from the diasporan press that on the occasion of events in Artsakh the three political parties [of the diaspora] have set aside their differences and reached a common understanding.[1]

---

[1] The three Armenian political parties founded prior to the Genocide did issue Joint Statements on a few occasions in the Ottoman and Russian empires prior to the First World War.

Finally. Those of us in Armenia thirsty for justice and concerned about the depletion of strength and need for reserves, we congratulated each other.

But what a disappointment to see [that what you had produced] was a rehash of appeals received from the "Soviet Union."

This is when we said, "As if our pain wasn't enough, now you have become a pain yourself." What can we do? You merely accelerated [the process of] our assessment of your [position].

As if there was no other way you could have made your existence felt in Armenia. Months after the beginning of major events inspired by [our love] of our people [in Armenia] your "national leaders"[2] sat around a round table, measured the good and the bad in Marlboro smoke-filled rooms and outlined their position with regard to events taking place in Armenia and to *Hayastantsis*[3] living critical times.

The Armenian Revolutionary Federation [Dashnaktsutiune] is adding its once virile voice to those of the leftover Hunchakians and Ramgavars.

And that is being done by signing a document which condemns the tactics of our struggle.

The Hunchakian and Ramgavar practice to please Armenia's overlords for seventy years are quite well known to all.

But you, Dashnaktsutiune, at least you should have had organizational self-respect; you should have avoided placing yourself in the position of a state prosecutor, by having "proven" guilt that does not exist . . .

You, who has led struggle for freedom worthy of books, you should have at least displayed respect for those from your ranks that sacrificed their lives in Khanasor[4] and the Ottoman Bank.[5]

---

[2] The expression "national leaders" does not convey in English the connotation of the Armenian term *"azgayin jojer"* which is a reference to the title of one of nineteenth century satirist Hagop Baronian's works. The characters in that volume are parochial petit bourgeois personalities who, involved in minor community projects and acting like "boss"es, believe themselves to be leading the nation.

[3] The Armenian word for "Armenian" is hay; it applies to all Armenians. Armenians call Armenia "Hayastan." The term *"Hayastantsi"* (Hayastan*ian*) is used to distinguish Armenians of Armenia from those in the diaspora. The use of the term is also an echo of the nineteenth century derogatory use of the term by the urbanized Armenians of Istanbul to describe the provincial and less educated rural Armenians of historic Armenia. The populist clergyman Mkrtich Khrimian tried to make people see the word as a positive definition, as an Armenian who had not left his fatherland.

[4] The "Expedition of Khanasor," a valley in Western Armenia, was a relatively large scale (300 participants) punitive guerrilla operation, mounted by the Dashnaktsutiune in 1896, against a Kurdish tribe that had participated in

How can you cover your shamelessness with cow's hide, when in order to assassinate the Sultan your own founder, Kristapor Mikayelian, gave his life experimenting with a bomb.[6]

Go ahead, condemn [us], talk to the Bulgar Communists, let them throw down the gorge from the mountain Vidosh the monument to our apostle.[7] Wasn't he the father of our position today, the mystifying teacher of our unusual will to give and devote oneself to the people?

We have no expectations from you, but on moral grounds, we would ask that you respect the memory of the unselfish dead.

You moved around the world without a fatherland, and you were able to keep your ethnic identity only. But you were created to be the flagbearer of the the revolutionary expression of your people and to exclude no tactic in the course of a struggle. But what do we get? Today you are signing a treaty against the strikers of Armenia along with the Hunchakians who were born out of anti-national "isms" and who now parade as nationalists[8] and with the Ramgavars who are still looking for their birth certificate.[9] Perhaps, while formulating this "historical statement," you were concerned that your own rank and file may follow the example of their brothers in Armenia.[10] [...]

There is more. Perhaps you are insulted that on the question of Artsakh we did not ask your opinion, and to resolve our just cause we did not ask for means of support from you.

It was not coincidental that one of the members of the Bureau, "armed" with the useless programs of struggle imposed upon us, witnessing the Zvartnots tragedy, ran to the Veharan[11] breathlessly, to complain, "Your Holiness, these Armenians have

---

the killing of Armenian freedom fighters. It is an event still occasionally celebrated every July.

[5] See Document One, note 21.

[6] See Document One, note 22.

[7] The mountainside cemetery in Bulgaria where Kristapor Mikayelian's grave is located. See Document One, note 28.

[8] Refers to the Marxism which the Hunchakians considered the basis of their ideology.

[9] Refers to the numerous times the Ramgavar Party has undergone name changes and composition. It may also refer to the fact that, as its stands now, the Ramgavar Party was organized in 1921, when major events defining Armenian history in the twentieth century were over.

[10] The Dashnaktsutiune prides itself in the discipline it imposes on its members. Despite its principle of decentralization, power is concentrated in the executive Bureau which has left little authority in the hands of regional executives and members.

[11] The building that houses the catholicosate.

lost their minds, they are throwing stones on the Russian soldiers."[12]

And this is being said by a leader of the Dashnaktsutiune.

Poor Dashnaktsutiune. Wouldn't it have been better if one of those stones directed at the armed Russian soldiers had hit you, so that you would wake up and your bourgeois . . .

No, and no. You were the master of the tricolor. But in a Soviet Yerevan turned Daltonic,[13] you were seeing red in flags that had become tricolor.

It is incomprehensible to you that the *Hayastantsi* considers the tricolor the flag of its last [independent] statehood and made it its own. And you, instead of feeling pride inside of you that, rather than fly in miserable club halls, the flag is flying in your real fatherland, that millions are now in solidarity with your persecuted loneliness,[14] you, afraid of these numbers, making noises in your hide out, you want to silence this [lion's] roar caused by those throwing arrows at us.

As if those condemning us were so few . . . and now from the other side of the ocean, you are trying to accuse us . . .

. . . Do you realize under what circumstances and within what context you are assuming the role of the accuser? But aren't you Armenian and under your wrinkled faces loom the condemning glance of your forebears? It may be that all of that seems unimportant to you, since in your strategy of retreat and to please alien forces you have adopted a non-Armenian path.

Having waited for six months, you now are concerned about the lives of workers being threatened by strikes.

It's a good thing *Hayastantsis* did not appeal to you for material help. For sixty years now, you lived many moments of humiliation in foreign lands, not having your own land under your feet. Under such circumstances [it is understandable] that your noble efforts at preserving your ethnic identity would be laced with the fatal poison of insecurity. [It is understandable] that after three generations, the fighting spirit is diluted. For sixty years you lived in peaceful and comfortable conditions. During those same years the *Hayastantsi* went through everything imaginable: A second holocaust in 1937, 300,000 young Armenians killed in the Second World War, widespread exile to Siberia in 1949. But the Armenian persevered; during those man-eating years he further refined his dignity, and with clenched fists produced the first fighting Armenians to defend justice. In the

---

[12] An incident when Soviet soldiers opened fire on peaceful demonstrators.

[13] Refers to color blindness.

[14] For decades the Dashnaktsutiune was singled out by Soviet and Soviet Armenian authorities as a target of attacks and ridicule for its role in the establishment of the independence of Armenia in 1918 and the exiled party's continued belief in independence.

1960s tens of young Armenians broke a forty-year silence and had the courage to defend the cause of our people, particularly your just cause.[15] That defense was rewarded with years in prison and the echo of your passive assessment.

And now, during these crises-filled days, with naive haste, you are trying to fix the conductor's baton between your fingers. And you want to teach us a lesson, excited by the *"Kun eghir balas"*[16] set on the podium. The thought has not occurred to you that a whole nation is getting ready to sing *"Pamp Orodan."*[17]

---

[15] Reference to the demands during soon-suppressed demonstrations in Yerevan in 1965 that the government of Armenia recognize the Genocide and claim Western Armenian territories. The Genocide is often regarded as an issue related to Western Armenians, i.e. the diaspora. That view is challenged by the recognition that a very large number of Armenians of Armenia, perhaps 50%, are of Western Armenian origin, including most members of the Karabagh Committee, if one goes back far enough in history.

[16] The most popular Armenian lullaby, "Be Asleep My Child."

[17] A militant song from the nineteenth century foreshadowing the rise of a revolutionary movement.

Appendix B

The Idea of Independence and Its Protectors

Appendix B-One

KHAJAK TER GRIGORIAN

Toward the Dawn of Freedom With an Independent Politics

The diaspora played a special role in the political culture of Armenia. The diaspora was a link with the nation's undistorted past and with the best that the West had to offer. From that perspective, the Dashnaktsutiune was seen as the most important among the diaspora organizations.[1] It had been the most daring and imaginative of pre-Genocide political groups; it had played a leading role in the establishment of the first republic in 1918; and it had continued to maintain that independence was a prerequisite for the attainment of national rights in the diaspora, while contributing to the organization of the new communities made up largely of survivors of the Genocide. The Dashnaktsutiune had a mystique in Armenia with which others could not compete.

In the diaspora, the Dashnaktsutiune was only one side of a community divided in half. The division, based on attitudes regarding independence and Soviet Armenia, were so sharp that it required little effort for the superpowers to manipulate the sides and lead them to intercommunity violence in the 1950s.

The end of the Cold War became a turning point for diasporan parties as well. The Dashnaktsutiune, like the others, realized that a national agenda requires freedom from ideological rigidity and from strategies that depend on ideologies, particularly when the ideology in question is a cover up for another state's interests.

This newly discovered attitude was reflected in a large number of articles, editorials, and speeches by leading members of the Dashnaktsutiune. Khajak Ter Grigorian, a scholar and member of the Bureau at the time this article was written, was one of the best representatives of the new thinking. The following document articulates a position which, in terms almost identical to Rafael Ishkhanian's

---

[1] See Document One, notes 19 and 63.

(Document One), reflects an evolution that must be seen as natural for the Dashnaktsutiune. In summary, Ter Grigorian argues that colonial mentalities tend to distort the perception of national interests, and reliance on others to execute the Armenian national agenda has produced no results. This argument parallels the views presented by Rafael Ishkhanian (Document One); similarities between the two extend even to the historical examples on which the arguments are based.

The document consists of excerpts from an article published in the May 13, 1987 issue of the Dashnaktsutiune Bureau organ Droshak, *on the occasion of the sixty-ninth anniversary of the establishment of the independent republic in 1918.*

[. . .] A close look at the current phase of the liberation struggle of peoples—whether directed against foreign rule or domestic exploiters—reveals a beautiful picture, which has been tainted at spots [. . .]

[We see] a people that has come out against the yoke of the foreigner, to destroy the chains placed on its hands and feet by imperialists, colonialists, and expansionists [. . .] The picture is beautiful [. . .] But it has been tainted by alien elements and one senses in it the presence of the foreigner's hand.

Unfortunately, a certain modus operandi has acquired the power of law for some and strategic value for others, all exceptions aside. According to this modus operandi, the leaders of peoples in the arena of the struggle extend their hands to this or that state and ask for their help, demand arms, ammunition and money, arguing that such requests are necessary for the success of the struggle. Occasionally, leaders and organizations first create alliances with the foreigner, receive its help, and only then appeal to their people to rise up. Let us not even discuss leaders and organizations born at the suggestion of the foreigner [. . .]

Such struggles are not merely devoid of beauty and noble characteristics; they also transform and distort realities and do not serve at all the goal of changing the status of their people. If the exploiters and oppressors were formerly the West, the Unites States and England, that function has now been passed on to the East, the USSR and its satellites. Such leaders of struggles are simply satisfying their passion for power and disregard the interests of the people [. . .] The people continue to be exploited. The chains, once on their hands and feet, continue to make their weight felt. The chains weigh on the tongues and brains [. . .]

[. . .] One must distinguish the above from the alliance and joint struggles of non-free peoples against imperialism, colonialism [. . .] Assistance between those who share the pain and fate cannot end up with the supremacy of one and the enslavement of the other; but the result of the alliance between the fox and the sheep is like wool thrown into the wind.

The struggle is beautiful when the fighter relies on its own strength, with self-confidence [. . .] It is beautiful, when the people waging the struggle determine the course of action in a sovereign manner and design their strategy independently [. . .]

Of course, some people will shrug their shoulders skeptically and ascribe the tenets of those who believe in an independent policy to an imagination derived from idealism. To these, we must paraphrase Jesus and ask, "You skeptics, why the ambivalence?" Isn't ambivalence in politics the start of and the door to opportunism and aimlessness? Open your eyes, look at the history of the community of men, look at the present and examine the situation from the point of view of peoples' interests and you will realize that struggles that rely on the power and help of foreigners—notwithstanding the cosmetic cover and propaganda type rationalizations—have been unable to deliver to their people the much sought after freedom and easing of the yoke.

[. . .] Poor people! As long as, in determining your orientation, you go back and forth along the path of ambiguities and ambivalences leaning on the interests of the foreigners, you are condemned to carry on your hands and feet the chains of domination. As long as you have not freed yourself from the common prejudices regarding orientations, as long as you are not relying on your own and independent strategy derived from your own interests, don't ever expect to greet the dawn of freedom.

[. . .] Skepticism toward an independent politics has unfortunately found fertile ground among a variety of Armenian groups with differing political perspectives, thus "filling water" in the mill of other powers and increasing the weight of the burden shouldered by the Armenian people.

Despite the strategy clearly designed by the Armenian Revolutionary Federation [Dashnaktsutiune] and a sovereign politics based on that strategy in connection with the liberation struggle of the Armenian people, there are still people—prejudiced, slavish people enthralled by the power of other countries—who, through shortsighted thinking, see the liberation of the Armenian people as being preconditioned by an alliance with the West or the East. The point of departure of this approach is not the interests of the Armenian people but rather their own subjective whims, their unfounded biases, and generalizations based on their personal interests.

The Armenian capitalist, [. . .] continuing to feel the impact of Western propaganda, equates socialism to Soviet communism and Bolshevism. And as a consequence, he has an antagonistic position toward the Soviet Union and, unconsciously—at times consciously—ends up in the lap of Western or American imperialism, seeing the prospect of Armenian liberation from a Western perspective [. . .]

There are also those among the opponents of an independent politics who admire the Russian "orientation" of Israel Ori[2] or Bishop Arghutian,[3] who feel glorified by the words of a character in Khachatur Abovian's work—words blessing Russian arms by an author persecuted by the Russian state—and who end up ascribing to Armenians an "eternal alliance" with Russia[4] [. . .] So much slavishness, so much sophistry, so much prejudice [. . .]

[. . .] There is no sphere of reconciliation between freedom and tyranny. The victory of one is conditioned by the defeat of the other [. . .] Therefore, any attempt on the part of a people involved in a struggle for liberation to have a rapprochement or alliance with the knights of tyranny is a sharp blow which destabilizes the foundations of independent politics [. . .]

Not only throughout history but in our own period, there have been so many peoples who, relying on their own strength and iron will to live in liberty, have been able to defeat foreign militaristic oppressors and their own power hungry overlords; [they have been able] to crush the tyrannical hand of highly industrialized forces endowed with the most advanced technology, and to achieve freedom and independence [. . .] That is real power.

[. . . We should not allow] the skeptics to frighten us with the military power of imperialist and expansionist states, like scarecrows in distant fields [. . .][5]

[. . .] The political history of the Armenian people also offers us similar examples. During the early and developed phases of feudalism, Armenia was often an arena of war where the East and the West clashed. And at times of peace each side would try to impose its influence in Armenia through local forces affiliated with them. For that reason, princes who were either shortsighted or bought out would see the guarantee of their own power in the swords of the foreigners and they would lean, wittingly or unwittingly, toward this or that foreign power, thus dividing the leadership of Armenia into two antagonistic parties. Only a small number of leaders, and only occasionally, were successful in resisting and determining their position inde-

2 See Document One, notes 7, 9, and 10.

3 See Document One, note 11.

4 See Document One, note 15.

5 The reference is certainly to Pan-Turkism discussed in similar terms by Ishkhanian (Document One, note 6). See Appendices B2, C-1, C2, and C3.

pendently. When the latter were able to benefit from the internal dynamism of the people, then it would be possible to change the course of history in favor of national interests. A Vahan Mamikonian,[6] a Hovnan Khutetsi,[7] an Ashot Yergat,[8] a Hetum[9] or Davit Bek,[10] even a Pilartos[11] or Gogh Vasil[12] were able to return freedom to their people when they were basing their strategy on sovereign politics. It is important to look closely at those incidents before and after Davit Beg. The vista that opens up to the researcher indicates that when the Israel Oris and Joseph Emins, who assumed the mantle of liberators of the Armenian people, relied on foreign powers and foreign intervention, they were unable to translate the inherent dynamism of the people into a pro-active force, while Davit Bek, relying on the capabilities of his own people, was able to return the freedom to Sunik. Unfortunately, his successors did not have the same farsightedness [. . .]

[. . .] The Armenian people have held strongly to their national consciousness [. . .] and a majority of Armenians reject any packaged and ready-made ideology. The goal of achieving a free and independent existence remains the focus of concern of Armenian masses.

Opposing these principles, ideas, and goals are the imperialist and expansionist powers. The diasporan segment of our people that escaped the racist sword of Turkey today lives in foreign countries, having been uprooted by force from its own land [. . .]

The fate of Armenians is not that different in Soviet Armenia [. . .] Even if not massacred and uprooted, its collective patrimony has been taken away by the presence of the foreign hand, the wealth representing common property has been looted, the thought and conscience of our people have been subjected to [state] terrorism, and our people have been denied fundamental liberties. Within these objective conditions every initiative undertaken by the people there toward a liberation struggle is a tactical step derived from the will of the people to live free and without constraints.

---

[6] Fifth century nobleman who led a rebellion against Persian rule.

[7] Ninth century leader of rebellion against Arab domination.

[8] Early tenth century king of the Bagratuni dynasty who led a popular defense of Armenians against invaders.

[9] Probably refers to thirteenth century king of Cilicia who attempted an independent and unorthodox policy of alliance with the Mongols.

[10] See Document One, note 13.

[11] Eleventh century Armenian ruler who attempted to resurrect the Armenian state based on a popular army and was partially and briefly successful.

[12] End of eleventh-early twelfth century rebel prince in Cilicia.

Thus, the goals of Armenians in the diaspora and in Armenia acquire a common denominator when the goal of freedom becomes an all-national one.[13]

[13] Compare to similar conclusion formulated by Vazgen Manukian at the end of Document Four.

Appendix B-Two

HRAIR MARUKHIAN
We Must Cherish the Vision of a Free, Independent, and United Armenia

> *The author of this document is the chairman, or representative, of the Bureau of the Dashnaktsutiune. Hrair Marukhian is undoubtedly the main architect, or the one most responsible, for the current policies of the Dashnaktsutiune.[1]*
>
> *The article from which the following was excerpted appeared two weeks after the previous document by Ter Grigorian, in the May 27, 1987 issue of the same publication, Droshak. This article too is on the occasion of the sixty-ninth anniversary of the establishment of Armenia's independence. Both precede the eruption of the "Karabagh" movement in Armenia; both were written after the possibilities of glasnost and perestroika were becoming obvious. The two seem to agree on the idea of independence but not on priorities and function of independence. The implications of what follows, while now revealed as Dashnaktsutiune policy, seem to counter the fundamental positions taken by the first. For Ter Grigorian, a national strategy not based on independent thinking, independent strategy, and independence is an abhorrence, and is certain to fail. For Marukhian, independence undergoes a process of mystification after which it becomes the last item on the national agenda, to be cherished only as an ideal, i.e. as a slogan useful for diasporans with identity crises.*

Freedom is the precondition for the multifaceted and harmonious development of the individual and social group alike [. . .]

Nations have equated their vision of freedom with their right to be free and independent. And based on such a vision, freedom fighters and revolutionaries of all times have carried the banner of revolt against oppression [. . .]

---
[1] See also Document One, note 62.

Despite the most unpropitious geopolitical conditions and difficulties almost unmatched by their scope, the Armenian people have struggled against expansionist powers and have fought relentlessly against competing powers that have forcibly turned the future of Armenians to a bargaining chip [. . .]

The realization of an independent state on May 28, 1918, was a historically significant date in the history of the Armenian people's struggle to achieve their rights; beyond that, it is the life-renewing and life-inspiring evidence which characterizes the crystallization of the national *credo* of the Armenian people [. . .]

And today, when the Armenian people are facing the current reality of Armenia on the one hand, and the reality of the Armenian diaspora on the other hand, when the [. . .] conflicting military and political interests may wear out those Armenians struggling to achieve their goals, when the Genocide of the Armenians committed by Ottoman Turkey continues to wreak havoc with the indirect complicity of those states which once condemned it, when even the friends of the Armenian Cause refuse to bother with it because of "high politics," today, at great sacrifice, the Armenian people must continue to adhere to the credo that was consecrated by the blood of one and one half million victims and by the lives of all those who died during the liberation struggle, and [see] the credo as the source of renewing energy, an impetus for the continuing struggle.

That credo is the guarantee for the complete freedom of a free and sovereign people. Therefore it must find its place in the hearts and minds of Armenian masses to give a qualitative depth to the ideological movement of Armenians at the forefront of the struggle for the demand of our rights.

That credo should press Armenians, now on the course of assimilation, toward a stronger national identity and self-knowledge.

That credo must unite its inherent potential to the gravitational power of the positive achievements of present-day Armenia and must direct toward our small nation the possibilities of Armenia so that the Armenia of today, which is anchor to tomorrow's united and independent Armenia, continues to grow and become a considerable power.

This credo—despite the logic of the argument that under the circumstances expounding on the subject may create difficulties in present day Armenia and may in no way serve the interests of our people—is one of those fundamental factors that in the present phase of Armenian history entail a mission of historic proportions. That mission is also favorable to our interests in the sense that it repels from the Armenian masses the sapping psychological state of co-optation, and not necessarily in the sense of opposing the present reality of Armenia, but rather, in continuously keeping within the field of political vision of all

Armenians that credo, whose mystique can have a much stronger centripetal force that would keep Armenians now spread throughout the world, bonded to Armenia.

At the same time, it is understandable that the realization of independence as part of a strategy for phased achievements borne out of realism may be the ultimate or penultimate phase. This [prioritization] further underlines the fact that the demand for independence is not necessarily the same as opposition to the present reality of Armenia. But this realism cannot mean that in the struggles of Armenian masses we may not take into account the inspirational importance of the idea of independence and consider the expounding of this highest of the national ideals, albeit an ideal whose realization may be actualized in the distant future, a "forbidden fruit."

Appendix C

Pan-Turkism, Democracy, and Independence

Appendix C-One

Pan-Turkism and the Armenian Question
The Twenty-Fourth World Congress of the Dashnaktsutiune

> The twenty-fourth World Congress of the Dashnaktsutiune convened in the summer of 1988.[1] At the conclusion of the Congress the party issued a communique regarding its deliberations. The following excerpt addresses the question of Armenia's relations with its neighbors and the basis of its association with Russia. Pan- Turkism appears to be the main context within which Armenia's interests are defined. While reaffirmed as ideals, aspirations such as democracy and independence are necessarily overshadowed by the perceived threat to national survival.
>
> This excerpt is from the communique published in translation in the May 1989 issue of Droshak.

[. . .] The most recent Armenian history is at a historic watershed. The Armenian Question has entered a new and decisive phase.

Of course, in essence, nothing has yet changed of the privileged position that Turkey enjoys amid the Western and Eastern alliances, a position which makes Turkey the main obstacle for the just solution of the Armenian Cause.[2] The United States of America and its allies, continuing to view Turkey as a barrier to the expansion of the Soviet Union and the widening of its sphere of influence, provides to the Turkish state extensive economic, military and social assistance. On the other hand, the Soviet Union, led by its own interests—among which an important consideration is the gradually developing Pan-Turanic dis-

---

[1] World Congresses normally convene every four years. They constitute the highest authority of the organization. It is the body that elects the Bureau, which assumes both executive and legislative authority during periods between World Congresses.

[2] For this statement to be correct, the Armenian cause must be defined strictly as a matter of the recognition of the Armenian Genocide and of Western Armenian territories, relegating to some undetermined position the questions of freedom, democracy, and independence.

positions linking the Turko-Tatar peoples inside its borders with Turkey—not only does not take a pronounced position against the ethnocentric Turkish state, but goes on further to court it periodically.[3] It is within this complex balance of conflicting powers that the Armenian people must operate towards the realization of its national political aspirations.[4]

[3] The complaint is the same as Balayan's. See Appendix C2.

[4] Such a definition places the Dashnaktsutiune in the tradition of those relying on the "third force," with all its implications for democracy and independence. This communique set the stage for the signing of the Joint Statement (Appendix A1); and for a significant speech made by chairman Hrair Marukhian in Vienna in November 1988, upon his return from Armenia where he met with then First Secretary of the Communist Party of Armenia, Suren Harutiunian. The hour long lecture on the situation in Armenia avoided all reference to the Karabagh Committee and the political struggle then underway. It focused on the need to leave politics aside and concentrate on Armenia's economic development. The chairman did make a point of his visit to the border with Turkey which led him to realize the problematic and questionable desirability of independence. The leader of the party of independence did not explain then or later why independence was seen feasible and desirable in the past, or how it would be possible in the future, since Turkey has been in the same location for some time and was not likely to displace ITSELF in the foreseeable future.

This was a strange position for the party that had symbolized freedom of thought and action, and independence, especially when the people of Armenia had undertaken a mass movement with the determination to achieve goals which it considered vital to its interests.

Questions and criticisms abounded from within and without. In the December 7, 1988 issue of the *Droshak*, the editor of the party organ Nazaret Berberian attempted to explain and defend the leadership position against criticisms. The article reads, in part:

"[. . .] We must stay away from all dissident extremisms and all adventurous positions which may lead to the dangers of anti-Sovietism and anti-Russianism, the realization of this priority being a target of the current phase of 'unification of Armenians' and 'unification of lands' [. . .] See Document Five, note 17.

At no time did we ever try to undo the Soviet state. Even at the height of the Cold War, our purpose was to make our voice heard from within.

It is true, in the process of determining its position vis à vis the Soviet side, the Dashnaktsutiune has passed through such phases when anti-Soviet dispositions and expressions registered marked increases. It is also true that our press has waged an unswerving and ideological battle against those steps by Soviet authorities that are directly against the interests of our people and in general against its totalitarian manifestations. But such statements by the Dashnaktsutiune have never led to a strictly anti-Soviet struggle nor a policy aimed at its disintegration [. . .]

Soviet Armenia—with its healthy people, intelligentsia, and state leadership that march along the path of Armenian national politics—constitutes the departing point of our strategy in the current phase of the Armenian Cause, as the anchor for the making of a united Armenia and united Armenians [. . .]

The Dashnaktsutiune has a whole historical experience that justifies its strong attachment to the conclusion that above all we must cherish the strategy of making Armenia and Armenians, along with its Soviet regime, the starting point of our struggle for the Armenian Cause [. . .]"

Appendix C-Two

ZORI BALAYAN

The Threat of Pan-Turanism

During the June 23-25, 1989, session of the Armenian Supreme Soviet (during the old regime) the role of Pan-Turkism in Armenian political thinking came to the surface. Zori Balayan pronounced a major speech in which he rearticulated his belief that Pan-Turkism[1] is the main threat to Armenia as well as to Russia, a threat that constitutes Armenia's common interest with Russia. Balayan was one of the original members of the Karabagh Committee, when the Committee's agenda was still limited to the question of Karabagh.[2]

The speech, delivered in Russian, was translated and printed widely. The following was excerpted from the July 12, 1989 issue of Haratch *.*

[. . .] It is sufficient to look into the folds of history. [. . .] One thing is clear: the Armenian and Russian peoples have together shed blood against the common enemy in order to see Armenia enter the structure of a unified Russian state.[3] And Armenia did enter that state (rather, a part of historic Armenia), by escaping from the fatal and barbaric Ottoman rule.[4] As the great Stasov has written, Armenia did not enter the Russian Empire empty handed. Rather it brought its share of a legacy of culture, architecture, social thought, and strategy.[5] Thousands of

[1] See Document One, note 6.

[2] See Document One, note 5.

[3] The speaker seems to disregard the political aspects of Armenia's annexation to Russia (See Document One, note 11). The assumption underlying this argument is, of course, the core of the debate. If there is a Pan-Turkic threat and if that threat is the gravest problem Armenians are facing, democracy and independence become secondary considerations.

[4] Eastern Armenia was under Persian Safawid rule when it was made part of Russia following the Russo-Persian War of 1827-28.

[5] Vladimir Stasov (1824-1906) was a Russian cultural figure who wrote extensively on the Caucasus.

revolutionaries from Armenia, especially Artsakh and, specifically its historic ancient capital Shushi, served Lenin's army. But Armenia could not even have imagined that soon after the October victory Kars, Artahan,[6] Sarighamish, Erzerum and the biblical mountain itself would be turned over to Turkish claws,[7] while Karabagh and Nakhichevan[8] would be given, with Stalin's help, to the newly created Muslim administrative structure.[9]

What then was the result? Our forefathers shed blood to remain within the Russian structure, but soon the grandchildren appeared outside Russia. Because if Azerbaijan exercises its constitutional right to secede on the basis of Article 72, then (what a surprise) it will take Nakhichevan and Karabagh along with it. Then what will our answer be to those who shed blood together? What will we answer to our forefathers who put forth the slogan "Forever together." Didn't the century fall short?

It is time to declare to the whole world that the Armenian people do not have now, nor can they ever have, religious intolerance toward others. The fate of our people has been such that we ended up at the crossroads of caravan routes. And the world now knows that by being the first to adopt Christianity,[10] Armenians simultaneously accepted and adopted also a universal principle that there are nine basic religions that constitute humanity's collective consciousness. No one has the right to impose a religion on another. We are grateful to the Muslim peoples of Central Asia, particularly to the Uzbek people, who provided sanctuary to hundreds of thousands of Armenians who had lived through the Genocide of 1918-1920.[11] We are grateful to the Muslim Arab world which saved hundreds of thousands of survivors of the 1915 Genocide. And it has been now four centuries that an Armenian community of a quarter million is flourishing in Iran where one finds an Apostolic church next to the mosque. And our two peoples, Iranians and Armenians, have come to realize fully that in the present world politics they must be allies. At the present time, we cannot tolerate the

---

[6] See Document One, note 54.

[7] Kars and Artahan had come under Russian domination after the Russo-Turkish War of 1877-1878 and were largely part of the Republic 1918-1920. The treaties of Alexandrapol, Kars and Moscow reverted it to Turkey. Erzerum,under Ottoman domination, came under Russian control briefly during the First World War. The biblical mountain is a reference to Mt. Ararat.

[8] See Document One, note 75.

[9] Reference to Azerbaijan.

[10] See Document One, note 79.

[11] Reference to massacres of Armenian in Baku, Shushi and other parts of Karabagh.

spread of the premeditated and fictitious hypothesis that people were waving Iranian Islamic flags during the events of Fergana in Uzbekistan.[12] The flags there were of a different green, the flags of Pan-Turkism, in pursuit of very concrete aims. And the aims are the same as ever: To enter Turan,[13] now dubbed Russia's "underbelly," going from Nakhichevan and the plains of Karabagh, by wiping out Mountainous Karabagh, using Meghri[14] as a highway. Isn't it time to think that we are now facing Hamlet's question: To be or not to be? Today the question is posed to Armenians; tomorrow Russia must face the same question.

Have you considered the question of why the Uzbeks who, at critical periods, have given refuge to Armenians, Crimean Tatars, Germans, Koreans, Georgia based Turks (while their capital Dashkent was seen by the civilized world as the city of bread that saved hundreds of thousands of orphans from the jaws of starvation), suddenly and without cause began massacring Turks? What happened? That is not how things normally work. Why is it that the grandfathers provided sanctuary and the grandchildren killed and burned homes? That is not the way things work, is it? That cruel task could not have been organized by Uzbeks, nor by Uzbekistan based Georgian Turks; after all, they are not masochists. We cannot allow ourselves to call the representatives of a whole nation masochists. [. . .] In Fergana we saw the realization of a Pan-Turkic aim. The aim of those who make Sumgaits happen. Probably very few are aware that at an agitated time of the Fergana events, members of the [Uzbek] Supreme Soviet received appeals from Metshkheti Turks to be relocated nowhere but in the Akhalkalak, Akhaltskha, and Bogdanova regions. But perhaps only the uninformed would pay attention to such geographic "trivia." These are exactly the regions where Armenians constitute a majority [in Georgia]. The fact is that Metskheti Turks have never lived in Javakhk[15] and that these regions are adjacent to the Armenian and Georgian republics. The purpose is clear: To surround Armenia by a Turkish noose. The same Armenia which, without [this noose], is already landlocked and blockaded. And this is the kind of provocation that is being carried out at the cost of the blood of innocent people. And then it is presented as the handiwork of hooliganistic elements.

---

[12] Reference to riots in Uzbekistan directed against residents of Turkish origin, Metskheti Turks, who originated in Georgia and were exiled to Uzbekistan by Stalin?.

[13] A term denoting a common fatherland in central Asia of all Turkic groups.

[14] The southernmost town of Armenia.

[15] Armenian historical name name for regions under discussion.

Karabagh is not just a geographic spot on the map. Karabagh is a provocation, an obstacle to the Pan-Turkic goal of reaching Turan, or Russia's "underbelly."

To be convinced that the fate of Nakhichevan awaits Karabagh, it is sufficient to be acquainted with but a small segment of the Pan-Turkic plan developed early on, by Nazim,[16] one of the leaders of the Young Turks: "In the Asian territories of the East, there are unlimited spaces and opportunities for development and expansion. Our forefathers have come from Turan (he has in mind Central Asia). And today throughout the Transcaucasus and on the other side of the Caspian Sea, toward the East, live Turkic speaking tribes, alas, under the occupation of our centuries old enemy, Russia. Only in that direction our political horizons lay free. And it is our sacred task to fulfill our obligation by achieving the union of Turkic tribes from the Mediterranean to the Aral Sea [. . .]"

The Pan-Turkic program was subsequently invested with new content. There appeared new slogans of the kind that said "Slow death to Nakhichevan," "Slow death to Karabagh," and, of course, slow death to Soviet Armenia. Incidentally, it also became clear that to execute the last slogan slowly but surely, it was sufficient to open a "private" highway through Meghri along the border with Iran to cut off Armenia from friendly Iran. For the leaders of Pan-Turkism, the conjunction of the terms "Armenian Statehood" has become loathsome. Why is it that the Russians, or more appropriately, the Soviet strategists were not aware of this?[17] One wonders how this could be, since it is written in black on white in the program [of Pan-Turanism]: "The existence of the Armenian state is the tombstone of our Pan-Turanic plans." And the latter, for Nazim, would constitute the death of Pan-Turkism. It is not incidental that he stated in Salonica: "Pan-Turkism must replace Pan-Islamism as the cornerstone of our policy since Pan-Islamism has lost its appeal and internal dynamism."

---

[16] A Young Turk leader, secretary of the Ittihad ve Terakke party during the First World War.

[17] See Document One, note 72.

Appendix C-Three

Pan-Turanism: A Response From the Karabagh Committee

> *The Karabagh Committee, noting how central the argument of Pan-Turkism is to the issues of democracy and independence, was quick to respond to Zori Balayan's speech on the floor of the Armenian Supreme Soviet (previous document).*
>
> *The statement was introduced and read by Levon Ter Petrosian. The translation of the statement is based on the text of the original as published in the July 12, 1989 issue of* Haratch.[1]

The Armenia Committee of the Karabagh Movement [Karabagh Committee] is deeply concerned with the antidemocratic character of the current session [of the Supreme Soviet] and with the fundamentally flawed and shortsighted political program presented there.

Based on the sense of responsibility which it has assumed on behalf of the aims of the Armenian people, the Karabagh Committee feels obligated to make the following statement from the podium of the highest authority in Armenia:

Despite our bitter experience, and disregarding the many disappointments our people have suffered, some of our intellectuals are still feverishly preaching the politically bankrupt and dangerous mentality according to which Armenia, being surrounded by enemy peoples of another religion, can survive only when it is under the protection of a powerful state. This mentality is leading our people to moral bankruptcy and denying it the opportunity to become a political partner, which is the only guarantee of success in political life. The concept of Armenia as an obstruction of Pan-Turanic plans and, therefore, as the political factor serving Russia's interests, pushes the Armenian ques-

---

[1] These statements on Pan-Turkism by Balayan and the Karabagh Committee were also reproduced in other Armenian papers. Most interesting were the editorial comments preceding their publication in *Droshak*. The organ of the Dashnaktsutiune praised the Balayan statement, although it took exception with the speaker's blanket statement on the absolute harmony between Armenian and Russian interests reaching back to the seventeenth century. The statement of the Karabagh Committee was said to include too many "dangerous ideas."

tion into the complex sphere of international relations, which has always been pregnant with dangerous consequences for our people.

As an ideology Pan-Turkism was born during the First World War and at the present has lost its value as a political factor, since Turkic-speaking peoples have opted for the path of national development. But crusader calls against it are apt to make it again a political factor and turn Armenia into a target of Pan- Turkism and Pan-Islamism.

The Karabagh Committee, leading the popular movement for over a year, has rejected from the start the dangerous mentality of placing our hopes on an external savior and seeing Pan-Turkism as a permanent threat. The Committee has labored systematically to act according to the principle that the Armenian people can achieve their national goals by relying on themselves, and only themselves. This political path has already produced obvious positive results by moving the Artsakh issue from the denial to the solution stage. Because of its just constitutional struggle, the Armenian people have made a number of allies within the international community: in Moscow, in Leningrad, in the Baltic republics, and among democratic forces. International support became possible because democratic forces appreciate the tangible role the Armenian movement played in the process of democratization in the Soviet Union. Secondly, relying on ourselves is the only guarantee of a just solution to the Artsakh problem, a solution we must cherish as we would the light in our eyes.

Conscious of this fact, forces that are pushing the Artsakh issue toward a dead end are organizing a grave conspiracy against our people, a conspiracy in which some of our intellectual elements are participating, wittingly or unwittingly.

The raising of the issues of Pan-Turkism and of the Armenian territories occupied by Turkey at this moment has only one purpose: to represent Armenians as revanchists, to discredit the just cause of Artsakh, and to deny Armenians the support of its allies.

For that reason, the Karabagh Committee condemns, in the harshest terms, the periodic attempt to turn the Armenian question into a cheap card within an international relations game. We are convinced that the only available path to achieve our national goals is to guarantee the irreversibility of the democratization of the country and the unity of the Armenian people on the principle articulated by the Armenian National Movement. We are convinced that had the ANM been formally recognized in time, and had there been an opportunity for an understanding between the leaders of the republic and the representatives of the people, we would have avoided the political adventure to which this statement is dedicated.

Postscript

Democracy, Diaspora, and the National Agenda

The following is the full text of the speech made by the editor at the Second Congress of the Armenian National Movement in Yerevan. With deletions and adjustments due to time constraints, it was presented on November 25, 1990, the third and final day of the Congress.

The popular and democratic movement in Armenia has introduced profound changes in the relations between Armenia and the diaspora. In its own way, the diaspora must now face the challenge which Armenia has already confronted over the past three years. My comments are personal and will refer largely to the situation in North American communities, although they seem to be relevant to other segments of the diaspora as well.

Initially, there was much in the movement that inspired the diaspora. The movement was sparked by the goal of reunification of Artsakh with Armenia, based on rights of self-determination and of nationalities. Largely a product of survivors of the depopulated regions of historic Armenia, the diaspora could not have remained indifferent to the plight of brethren in Artsakh who asked for no more than the right to live as a community and in dignity on their own land—and the right to choose the path toward achieving that dignity.

Secondly, a diaspora frightened by the direction of Armenian history saw in the Karabagh movement a turning point: The possibility of reversing the millennium old process of depopulation of the historic homeland, a process epitomized by the Genocide in Western Armenia and continued in Nakhichevan.

It was also the Karabagh movement that forced the government of Armenia in 1989 to recognize formally the Genocide of 1915. The Genocide is not the problem of the diaspora alone, of course. But it represented the core of the political, territorial, cultural and psychological issues the diaspora faced.

In a brief period of time, the movement became more than an accounting of the past and the present. Soon it became obvious that Armenians saw in Artsakh the symbol for the political, cultural, spiritual and economic revival of our nation; and the people of Artsakh saw in the movement a vehicle for the generation of the popular will to determine their own future. The Karabagh movement became the national movement as it became clear that neither the Karabagh issue nor the other questions on the agenda could be resolved within the existing structures.

The national movement was the first in long decades that gave us a sense that Armenians were *for* an idea, *for* a right as part of a realistic agenda; a sense that we could participate in history in a positive manner and that history was more than the hatred of the "Communist" or of the "Turk." For too long, history had become a spectator sport we watched from the sidelines. The political arena provided us merely a pulpit whence we issued moral condemnations of diplomats who "betrayed" us.

The combination of an honest accounting of the past and a vision of the future inspired by the universal rights of democracy and freedom did more to overcome the walls separating Armenia from the diaspora than decades of formal relations and exchanges. That which the movement, anchored in the people's most basic needs and aspirations, gave the diaspora may be impossible for the diaspora to repay. As a result of the movement, we have whole generations of Armenians, born in different countries, who no longer need to ask "What is an Armenian?" Because Armenians live and act as a nation, we no longer need to define them and, by so doing, limit their identity or treat them as a relic of the past. The movement gave the diaspora what it has been unable to achieve through an extensive chain of dedicated organizations and institutions. In this respect, the people of Armenia and the movement they created did more for the diaspora than seventy years of defensive battling or decades of occasionally successful but often embarrassing efforts at recognition by the international community.

And yet, the national movement in Armenia and Artsakh had a profoundly destabilizing impact on diaspora institutions and values. And it is not at all certain that we have appreciated all the dimensions of the movement or that our diaspora leadership has articulated fully the depth of support for the national and political regeneration which Armenia has undertaken.

Armenians in Armenia tend to see the diaspora as a monolithic entity, an undifferentiated structure that has internalized the best the West has to offer. Yet the diaspora is heterogeneous. And it changes, just as Armenia did during the past 70 years. Diaspora Armenians represent a spectrum of opinions, beliefs, and relations more varied and less amenable to rational organization than is the case in Armenia.

The diaspora has become very complex and fluid, even if one compares it with twenty years ago. For seventy years, communities and their dominant organizations have adjusted, sometimes imperceptibly, to host societies. Gradually, they have brought their agendas closer to the agenda of governments under which they live. Organizations and generations within each community have adjusted in their own way. These adjustments have been compounded by the disrupting, even if occasionally beneficial, effects of continuing waves of emigration and immigration that make the accumulation and transmission of experience from generation to generation or community to community difficult, if not impossible.

Underlying these differences is a characteristic which all diasporans share and which is the critical difference with Armenia. The diaspora, by definition, is the denial of nationhood, the absence of statehood, whether nationhood and statehood are defined politically or geographically.

Statehood, along with the problems and promises it holds—is the only category that could have transcended the important—and sometimes not so important—differences between Armenians with varying partisan, religious, clannish, or even esthetic allegiances. Even where we have been involved in state affairs, it has always been as a religious or ethnic minority, as a lobby, not as a participant in the building of a state, the making of history.

The diaspora is destabilized because it spent seventy years coming to terms with the former regime of Armenia, finding ways of compromising its own ideals. Mirroring our own lack of a sense of statehood, we learned to accept the regime by reducing the nation into an abstraction: Armenia for us became a museum that attested to our past, that fueled our need for cultural identity. Armenians in Armenia were the museum keepers. We asserted, almost with a sense of relief, that the Armenians of Armenia had no role to play in the making of history. We no longer recognized you when you acted as a living nation.

We thought we recognized ourselves in you when you raised the question of the reunification of Karabagh with Armenia. We too had been making demands for "Western Armenia" for decades. To equate the two, however, we had to reduce your cause to a "demand" like our: A demand from others and dependent on others, at best as an act of history-based justice, at worst an act of territorial expansion, always an act of mercy, not of democracy and self-determination; an act of master-vassal relations, not of the struggle of a sovereign nation. Just as a hundred years ago in the Ottoman Empire, or now in the diaspora, we elevated the fear of offending our masters to the level of principle. After all, how could we, if our survival depended on others?

Individual bravery came to replace collective political imagination as the stuff from which history was made. What we ended up seeing in history was patterns of conformity, opposition to change.

We thought we recognized ourselves in you when you insisted on a formal recognition of the Genocide. We failed to see that you wanted to set history in order, to learn from it and build on it. As for us, the Genocide has paralyzed us; it denied us the normal processes of growth and maturation. At times it seems that there was nothing left to define us and distinguish us from others, other than our being the first victims of genocide in this century. The Genocide has become a negative form of self-definition. To paraphrase a friend, our death certificate has become our flag.

We were angry at the "Turk," for what he had done to us, and at the world, for wanting to forget what the Turk had done. So we reduced politics to a set of angry reactions. We were unable to develop frameworks of real participation in the affairs of the states in which we lived other than as supplicants. As the worthy inheritors of the *"millet"* mentality, we strove to remain "good" citizens and tend to our schools, churches, and clubs. Increasingly, politics consisted of securing a little recognition, a little safety.

At the beginning of the post-Genocide diaspora, we sought community life, cultural identity, and collective memory. This was a noble undertaking and a heroic effort for the surviving orphans in the early decades of diaspora formation. But this search was institutionalized and perpetuated in more recent decades as the fear and hatred of the Turk, the fear of assimilation. The memory of collective death became the fear of the future, the fear of one's neighbors: "Turkey is there to massacre Armenians any chance it gets" became the only political orthodoxy, and "*odars* (non-Armenians) are there to assimilate our young" was the cultural manifestation of the same debilitating notion. And since the diaspora was caused by the Genocide, somehow all our problems could be traced to the Turk, and we could absolve ourselves of any responsibility. After all, who among us would dare absolve the Turk of any guilt?

Here we see how the institutional values of the diaspora evolved parallel to those of Armenia and made possible the ultimate compromise the diaspora made with the former regime. In Armenia too it was the fear of the Turk that led to the consolidation of the power of the Communist Party. The Communist Party of Armenia was the intermediary between Armenia, the potential victim—the only way Armenians could see themselves in the international arena—and Russia or the USSR, the only possible protector. Democracy, human rights, and independence could not be on the agenda and leaders could not be blamed for not placing them on the agenda, as long as fear dominated our relations with the rest of the world.

Both in Armenia and in the diaspora, participation in that fear and hatred came to replace participation in collective thinking and decision-making. Reactions were confused with principles; promoters of fear and hatred became the strategists and perpetuated the collective paralysis. What was there to participate in, after all? If the question facing our nation is how to keep bloodthirsty and irrational Turkey and Turks from killing more of us, then the answer would be to seek a protector. The price of that protection is the loss of all other rights, including the right to question authority.

One cannot but understand the need of wandering diasporans to find some stability, the need to build a life with some sense of permanency, a sense of the future which their forefathers were denied and which they could build only for their children. But one must also understand the ability of intellectually clever and enterprising leaders who exploited the Armenians' natural needs to feel comfortable in their weariness of political life, equated participation with the writing of checks and ended by guiding them to the margins of history.

To move from a state of despair to the politics of symbolism and rituals did not require much imagination or intelligence in a diaspora still obsessed with recognition from the outside. To a nation turned refugees and denied its past, inducing an abdication of history and a denial of a future seemed almost a natural progression based on a strategy of fear and hatred.

Promising to resolve all the problems we face, our leaders reduced the national agenda to problems which could not possibly be resolved: the Genocide cannot be undone, Turkey will not disappear from the face of the earth, and assimilation in the diaspora is a matter of degree and time only. But we are witnessing the politics of symbols, rituals, and mystification. The grander the mystery, the more successful the politician.

We should have anticipated, perhaps, that the national movement's positive and realistic agenda would not only challenge the former regime in Armenia but also destabilize the diaspora's dominant value system, many of its institutions and leaders.

We should not have been surprised, probably, that a democratic movement would produce an instinctive antagonism which many of our leaders developed very early toward the movement. Isn't democracy, after all, the right to know, to debate, to critique and to challenge and, if need be, change government or leadership?

The questioning of authority and orthodoxy in Armenia could have inspired sufficient confidence in diasporans to ask some pertinent questions of their own: Has the much-heralded strategy of cultural preservation based on fear of the neighbor and on isolation produced results? Did a strategy of liberation based on anti-Turkism and anti-communism, on fear of Pan-Turkism and hatred of the Turk, cause the return of an inch of Western Armenian territory or bring us any closer to Turkish recognition of the Genocide? Did conditions in Soviet Armenia lead to the resolution of the outstanding issues on the national agenda? Did culture—the culture which we claimed to be preserving in the diaspora or recreating in Armenia—help or stymie the process of political thinking, debate on strategies, development of sovereign assessment of national interests, the use of our faculty of judgement?

Are these not, ultimately, the questions that must decide what worked and how to decide them? And have we not seen the repression of criticism in the name of imagined national interests, in the name of pseudo-strategies so fragile that they could not survive a little exposure, a little scrutiny?

It is one of the paradoxes of diasporan development that, of all the adjustments our institutions made to host societies in their quest for survival and self-preservation, democratization was not one of them. Respect and tolerance of rational discourse and others' opinions on the major issues confronting our people were not internalized and institutionalized in our community life. As a result, we have lost what capacity we had to accept criticism. Debate on goals and strategies, on successes and failures is characterized as weakening the fiber of our culture.

One cannot but juxtapose the secret politics of diasporan groups with the live television broadcasting of the proceedings of this congress. Here, under the most trying of circumstances, the shaping belief seems to be that information and debate are the bases of good government. Our political parties and organizations that currently define priorities and policies continue to prefer secrecy. In the diaspora, interests and positions are proclaimed rather than discussed; the right to speak on behalf of Armenians continues to be claimed as an entitlement rather than won democratically. The by-now counterproductive ideology of cultural self-preservation has degenerated into the self-preservation of an elite whose mandate is far from being clear, and into the perpetuation of mechanisms that might have been appropriate, at most, during the struggle against the Ottoman regime.

We may still understand, perhaps, why political parties, whose policies with regard to Turkey have failed, now demand that the democratic movement and the freely elected government of Armenia adopt the same policies. Diasporan political leaders do not feel they have a price to pay when they confuse organizational reflex with nation building, when they identify the fate of the nation with its representation in the media, when they equate anachronistic rhetoric with strategic accomplishment.

We could take pains to explain, perhaps, why diasporan political parties would latch onto the Genocide issue as the ultimate weapon against the democratic movement in Armenia. We can understand why the diasporan parties have misrepresented and misconstrued the position of the Armenian National Movement. The experience of the diaspora could have taught us that building a cultural identity and political activities around the Genocide can only lead to dead ends. And dead ends we have reached, otherwise how could we explain the mad rush of diasporan political parties to Armenia, when the account books on their diasporan strategies have not been closed yet. Yet rush they did, most of all to denounce the government for its assessment that the future and the foreign policy of Armenia cannot be built around the Genocide, that recognition of the Genocide cannot constitute the *sine qua non* of Armenia's outlook on its neighbors, that nation-building requires different rules than the building of clubs, that a government—especially a democratically elected government—has different responsibilities than a school board, that a state is not just another community institution to be controlled.

We can, perhaps, understand why all of this can happen.

But it is not so polite on the part of these leaders to claim that they speak for all diasporans or, as in one case, for all Armenians.

It is difficult to preach of democracy and disregard the principles of discourse and debate. One must suspend too much disbelief for too long, one must forget too much and too soon to reconcile with the claims of parties that their past failures constitute visions for a future.

Faced with such a radical challenge from Armenia as the national democratic movement, the organizational survival instinct produced in our diaspora a marriage of convenience between various parties and organizations. The guiding principle in that arrangement was the decision not to rethink issues, and to deny the depth of changes sweeping Armenia and the diaspora. Now we are expected to accept this cohabitation as a sign of maturity, when its most strident product was the infamous statement of the three parties in the fall of 1988 on the Karabagh movement and, more recently, the squabbling over the visit to the US last fall of Armenia's president.

The common interests of dominant elites within and outside Armenia have been obvious since the beginning of the movement but not limited to it. It seemed that the parallel extended to the logic of the now-ousted leaders of Armenia to turn the earthquake and the quest for economic development into tools of depoliticizing Armenians, to deny them the right to set their agenda, and choose their own leaders. Assistance for earthquake relief and economic development, however well intentioned and supported by the mass of diasporans, performed the function of telling Armenia that it could not help itself, that it must rely on outside help, and that, therefore, it had no right to make decisions. There were many moments when, for diaspora communities built by refugees of the Genocide, the assistance to victims of the earthquake was predicated upon viewing Armenia as a country of refugees. That seemed, for some, a more convenient, less troubling, less demanding relationship than one that required the diaspora to see Armenians claiming national and democratic rights and acting as a nation.

My purpose here is not to deny or minimize the contributions institutions have made in the past, continue to do so now, or have the potential to do in the future. Our political parties, and diaspora institutions in general, have played a historical role; they have served our people the best they could. Under trying circumstances, they have tried to help diasporan communities and Armenia. In many ways they have succeeded. And we can have nothing but respect and awe toward those who gave more than their share. For the generation that escaped death, it required a daring act of imagination to think that there would be other generations, that the other generations deserve to receive from the survivors something more than the memory of death.

We must, nonetheless, continue to scrutinize our situation now and rethink our attitudes. We must reassess our organizations and reorient ourselves.

The first factor regarding the reassessment of our organizations is that they are no longer what they were in 1887 or 1890, 1914 or 1918, 1920 or 1923. Particularly under the circumstances of diasporization, our organizations have changed, and they have changed to the point where their performance before the First World War is no longer an indication of the validity of their current policies. If age were the only source of experience and wisdom, or if survival were a guarantee for wisdom, one would have to question why political parties were even founded at the end of the last century instead of allowing the Church—a much older and more experienced institution—to continue defining the national agenda, policies, and identity. Revolutions become possible and necessary because situations change and yesterday's solutions become today's problems; they become necessary because institutions develop institutional egos to the point where reality is distorted and it is no longer possible to distinguish between problems and solutions.

The second factor is that social institutions, particularly in non-sovereign organisms, seldom define themselves. Their members can state goals and values, they can contribute the maximum of their abilities with those goals and values in mind. Yet their political significance, their impact on society and history are defined largely by the environment within which they are functioning. Our political parties too, with all their good intentions, have an impact beyond, and occasionally contrary to, their intention and their stated goals.

The third factor is that an organization can have a successful and acceptable policy—at least to its members—in one area or at one level, but that is not an adequate guarantee of its performance in another area or level. Community organization is both a type and a level of activity. Assuming we consider our diaspora organizations successful in this respect, they would still have no more preparation and experience to run a government, to build a disaster zone, or reform the economy of a state in which they have not lived.

History and, one hopes, civilized and open debate, will offer assessments of the role and impact of our organizations as time progresses. My concern is that in thinking of the future and of the participation of the diaspora in that future, we must take nothing for granted. We must now look at our diasporan values and structures in the context of new realities in the world, in Armenia, and in the environment within which Armenia must live and prosper. We must make sure we are addressing the right questions, we have the right agenda.

Clearly, we must ask some simple questions: To what extent and in what ways do diaspora organizations, especially political parties, represent diaspora Armenians? Do these organizations, as structured now and as they relate to each other today, represent the best mechanisms to channel the diaspora's contributions to the political and economic development of Armenia? Have these organizations reassessed their own experience and policies in view of the new situation and needs that have arisen?

What can be offered now are tentative answers. I would argue that at this point in our history institutions and organizations have not, by and large, risen to the occasion; they have not been able to articulate the values of an increasing number of diasporan Armenians who are no longer concerned with antiquated arguments; with obsolete disputes; with petty quarrels whose sole function seems to have been to distract attention from strategies too long taken for granted; with internalized aggression characteristic of the mentality of the colonialized; with the politics of rhetoric and fear; with the psychology of the victimized.

The once understandable strategy of cultural self-preservation has now degenerated into the strategy of equating culture with structures of cement and politics with short term tactical advantages, all consecrated by symbols that are by now quite ineffective.

The vitality of Armenians in Armenia, their courage in questioning the premises of seventy years of Soviet thinking, and their acceptance of hardships that will follow the pursuit of a new, democratic agenda have inspired the most active diasporans to seek avenues and methods of participation in the task of building Armenia. The question here is: Will this participation come in the form of emotional outbursts or a well thought out and rationally defensible plan? Have seventy years of cultural strategy and "politicization" in the Diaspora not produced a structure that can accomplish this? Can our dominant institutions stand a little criticism without branding those criticizing as heretics or traitors? Can they contribute to the building of a democratic nation?

Many continue to believe that our core institutions are the proper vehicle for this task. Yet what has transpired thus far does not inspire any confidence that this view is based on anything more than faith. For many of the faithful, it is difficult to imagine oneself outside the circle created by the tradition- and history-laden organizations; their identity is intertwined with such an association. In the absence of a state, this was only natural, even necessary for a sense of self- definition and identity.

However, when the people of Armenia produced the new agenda of nation building in Armenia and offered the opportunity to the diaspora to participate in a meaningful way, the current leadership failed to transcend the limitations of diasporan thinking and behavior and to join forces with the democratic movement of Armenia.

We, in the diaspora, should have the humility and courage to recognize that our institutions were not built to face the new, and bigger, challenges facing our nation; that in order for the diaspora to realize its great potential, our institutions must undergo actual transformations; that most of our crises thus far have been existential, dealing with insecure identities rather than with the strategic uncertainties; that the skills, know-how, talent, and capital which could contribute to the development of Armenia abound in the diaspora, but they abound in individuals—and talent can't be easily mobilized by undemocratic institutions.

Our political thinking has been meandering over the past seventy years, just as we, diasporans, have been moving from country to country. The movement in Armenia has helped many in the diaspora to reassess the diasporan political processes of the past twenty years. It is not uncommon to hear now the argument that the current diasporan strategy, while producing no territorial gain, has also pushed Turkey into making denial of Genocide an integral part of its foreign relations; accordingly, it has devoted the necessary academic and financial resources to the task, with some success.

The time had come to reassess the issues and policies of the past decades, to understand history and act in a way that makes real participation and real change possible; the time had come to distinguish between the real and the ritualistic. In the diaspora, words and claims have no impact on our economic and political survival. For diasporans, successes or failures affect our pride, our individual and collective memory, or the dignity attached to our ethnic identity. There we can claim successes and blame the rest of the world—or other Armenians—for our failures.

This may be adequate for the diaspora, but Armenia is not just another community and a state is more than just another community institution. Words, actions, successes and failures will make a difference in real ways on the real lives of a whole nation, and on the state that houses that nation. It is not possible to transfer the logic, the institutions and, above all, the mentality of a diaspora into Armenia. It is not possible to apply the principles of non-accountability, non-responsibility to Armenia. That is why the democratic dimension of the movement is essential to Armenia, and must be non-negotiable.

For the diaspora organizations to participate constructively in the making of Armenia's future, they must fully share in the democratic and national values being created by the people of Armenia and its movement. To have a right to continued leadership in the diaspora and before they can make a claim to leadership in Armenia, political parties must apply to their own past the same critical review which Armenians in Armenia applied toward their own past. Before they rebuild Armenia, they must assess what they have built in the diaspora, how they have used its resources, responded to its needs; where they have succeeded and where they have failed.

Before it can wear its age as a sign of strength, the Hunchakian Party must explain why it was possible to declare for decades that the Sovietization of Armenia represents the realization of all political dreams of Armenians. Before it can impatiently demand that the new government of Armenia lay claim to Western Armenian territories, the Ramgavar Party must explain why it could live without any such concerns for decades without feeling it was betraying national interests. Before it can use the issue of Genocide as a stick against the new government, the Dashnaktsutiune must explain how the party could be engulfed in the 1950s anti-communism of the Cold War for two decades that it would forget about Turkey. This most important of diaspora political parties must explain why it is that in November 1988 its leadership could ask everyone to dedicate themselves solely to issues of economic development of an Armenia governed by the Communist Party, thus helping extend the rule of the former regime and delaying the coming of democracy. But then, as a democratic government is elected, the party leadership reverses its stand, questions the legitimacy of that government, and seeks to replace it.

Before diaspora political parties can equate mere survival and experience, they must explain to themselves and to the nation why it was that their age and experience did not prevent them from becoming the tools of others' policies and led them to kill each other. That they are no longer killing each other is hardly a sign of maturity, if they are still unwilling to come to terms with the mentality and policies that brought upon such disasters to begin with. Parties and organizations must explain why, despite all the crises and opportunities of the last three years, there still is a divided church which, if united, could save enough resources to provide for the health needs of the children of Armenia.

Self-critique is essential not only for the elucidation of history but also to achieve a better understanding between Armenia and the diaspora; and to ensure the openness necessary for mutual trust. Above all, maximum cooperation and efficiency can be achieved when there is sharing of values. For the first time, the diaspora can be part of Armenia, because it can share without any reservations in the ideal of nation-building and the process of democracy.

Maximum cooperation and efficiency will remain idle expressions, if the diaspora's institutions continue to ignore the question of democracy, openness, credibility, and accountability, if they wish to continue to speak in the name of the diaspora. The example of the new leadership of Armenia, elected by the people, is telling: The new government can propose and discuss ideas and strategies which could not be publicly mentioned before because the people of Armenia have given them a new mandate, a mandate to redefine national interests, and to think and act boldly.

For the first time in a long time we, as a nation, have a positive agenda not based on the hatred and fear of the Turk. In order to contribute to Armenia's rebuilding, the diaspora organizations must learn to cope with an environment where hatred and fear do not dominate our nation's thinking. Only then can we open up the processes of deliberation and decision-making, instead of closing them as has happened during the past two years.

There are now new groups, smaller groups, that are coming together everywhere to fill the gap that is widening; groups that seek their legitimation in what they can do for the future, not in what they have done in the past; groups for whom the past is not a burden, a locked prison but a key—sometimes a painful one—to the future, and that can imagine new bases of association with the processes taking place in Armenia. History has a way of differentiating between those who merely survive and those who contribute; between those who can occupy space in the media and those who perform a constructive role for the future. A revamping of diaspora thinking is necessary not only to ensure that all organizations perform according to their rhetoric as far as Armenia is concerned, but also to make sure that the problems of the diaspora, as a diaspora, are not forgotten.

The Armenian nation faced a challenge in 1988. Armenia answered that challenge by democratizing and by setting a national agenda. The Diaspora has yet to take up that challenge. Our organizations, including political parties, which have done much in the past, have an opportunity to play a major role in the new age as well. For that to happen, they must take up the challenge, in the spirit that gave them their greatness many decades ago. They must, above all, transcend the limitations of diasporan life.

Our organizations and institutions count among them some of the most dedicated individuals of the community, people who have spent a vast amount of their personal resources to make these institutions work. Institutions must now adjust to their members, actual or potential, as they adjust to the new era.

Times are changing. It is the issues that determine the kind of resources needed and the form in which these must be organized. "Feeling" Armenian, feeling part of community, and real or symbolic gestures of personal sacrifice are no longer the criteria of measurement. When there is an agenda as large as nation-building, what matters are the actual results of the individual and collective actions we take, measured against the larger agenda.

We, diasporans, must grow with history or history will crush us. We must change even if change means having to rethink the compromises we have made with history by force of events, by force of diasporization. We must not, we can no longer afford to allow the Genocide and diasporization to dictate our thinking and agenda, as if we had no collective capability to use our reason and act on another basis than reflex, other than merely reacting to our past. We must rethink not only for the sake of Armenia but also for a healthy Diaspora.